Life On The Run:

Coast to Coast

Matt Beardshall

Published 2007 by arima publishing

www.arimapublishing.com

ISBN 978-1-84549-247-2

Printed and bound in the United Kingdom

Swirl is an imprint of arima publishing

arima publishing
ASK House, Northgate Avenue
Bury St Edmunds, Suffolk IP32 6BB
t: (+44) 01284 700321

www.arimapublishing.com

For Andrea, Hannah and William

Acknowledgements

My gracious thanks go to the following people, without whom the coast-to-coast adventure would never have become a reality:

The rest of the RespectTheStupidity team; - Mal Gibb, Vincent Vanwoerkom, Andy Farnsworth and Justin Adams, especially Andy and Justin who worked tirelessly in support of the idiots running and cycling.

Andrea, Hannah and William Beardshall for allowing me time to train and giving me leave of family duties to go on a running adventure for a week.

Ann and Roy Stocks, June and Geoff Beardshall, for being extremely helpful and supportive grandparents.

Mike "Mad Dog" Schreiber at www.training2run.com

Special Thanks to:
Andrea Lawton
Ans Vanwoerkom
Phil 'The Pill' and Sheena Clarke
The Red Bull drink company
Rachel at 'Gillercomb' in Rosthwaite

Also:
Comrades on the chat forum at www.coast2coast.co.uk
Colleagues in the Imaging Department at Chesterfield Royal Hospital
Alan Ward and Mick Heys
Ken Bishton
'U-Computer' computer services and internet cafe in Keswick
Everybody who sponsored our stupidity and pledged money for BBC Children In Need.

Prologue

19th November 2004

Vin and I had been sitting in the back of the car for half an hour and our shoelaces were still too frozen to be untied. The time was around 10:30 pm and the temperature gauge said it was minus 5 degrees outside. All four of us were in high spirits as we headed back to Chesterfield; Mal and Andy, in the front seats, had been our support crew for the run which had gone excellently well, and who now continuously plied us with hot tea and cakes on the journey home. We joked about how running up and down mountains in sub-zero conditions in the dark of a freezing winter night was probably not the best way to a long and pain-free life.

It was the Children in Need charity night, and our fun involved two of us running a half-marathon distance at night in November over the hills and moors in the Ladybower area of the Peak District. We'd driven past the village of Hope and parked in a little lay-by in the Edale valley. The car journey had been a fairly adventurous affair due to the recent weather conditions. Freezing temperatures for a few days followed by several inches of snowfall made for interesting driving along the narrow tortuous lanes. As the car stopped and the engine and lights faded we were struck by the intense silent darkness. Pinpricks of light from a few distant scattered farmhouses provided the only evidence of civilisation. Even the sublime tangerine glow of the major conurbations of Sheffield and Manchester could not permeate this deeply into the National Park. The silence wasn't to last long. It was too cold to hang around so Vin and I pulled on our Camelbak rucksacks (a backpack that contains a fluid reservoir and has a tube with a mouthpiece so that the wearer can drink whilst on the move) containing radios and minimal emergency gear, and donned head-torches whilst Mal and Andy laughed and mumbled words that sounded like "daft bastards". For an extra bit of rousing motivation *Carmina Burana* by Orff was blaring from the car stereo, resulting in bemused looks from a small group of hardy hill sheep we could just make out in an adjacent field. A quick photo shoot followed for posterity and we were off.

As usual Vin, 10 years younger, fitter and faster, set off like a whippet at a pace unsustainable by me as we headed up the climb onto Win Hill. The first mile or so of the route was on a wide rough bridle track. I could just see the reflective strips on Vin's running trousers as he quickly pulled away. Between gasps for breath I shouted that I had to slow down or I'd never make the distance. He heard and dropped back to join me, barely even breathing heavily. There was some ice and a little snow on the lower part of the climb that caused a few slips and a little jollity but nothing like we were to encounter further on.

Twenty minutes or so later we were on the top of the Win Hill plateau for one of those moments that stay with you forever. The sky had cleared completely and there were six inches of undisturbed snow on the ground that reflected the moonlight in an eerily beautiful way. We could see the mountains round us in all directions like giants lurking ominously in the shadows. We were able to switch off our head-torches and run swiftly by the light of the moon as it lit up our way, the only sound being the pleasing crunch of crisp new snow under every footstep. The air was cold and refreshing as we sucked it in, and it felt like we could have run this way forever. Every few steps clouds of shimmering ice crystals danced round us like a mini-firework display as we kicked through deeper patches of snow on the uneven ground. It was sublime until the radios crackled and we heard "weyyy-heyyyyyyy". Clearly Mal and Andy were having fun in the car somewhere in the icy valley as they drove to the first rendezvous point on the Snake Pass road. The plan was to meet them after dropping down a steep and rocky trail that we knew well having biked it numerous times. Tonight it was not only steep and rocky but also more resembling of a glacier, the stream that sometimes runs down it having frozen into a sheet of ice several inches thick through which the rocks protruded like instruments of medieval torture. In an instant the run went from beautiful to dangerous, and the pace slowed considerably. Here I was to get my own back on Vin. Downhill is more my scene and, as he had also chosen a head torch with half the power of a candle, I sped away from him. Every few minutes one of us would slip and take a painful fall but somehow this added to the fun. Mal and Andy were in position and could see our lights descending. A few times they called on the radios but we were too busy trying to stay upright and alive to call back. We safely navigated our way down and jogged over to the car, all four of us laughing like idiots.

The first leg of the run completed, the support guys offered us hot drinks and refills for our Camelbaks. We declined and set off straight away before thoughts of sitting in a warm car and drinking tea took hold. The next leg was to take us over Lockerbrook Farm, through the woods and down to Ladybower for another rendezvous. Another big climb started and again I watched Vin disappear up into the distance. Half way up the climb it became a little surreal as, one by one, groups of young children, each with an adult, appeared, walking down the mountain towards the road. "Evening," they all said merrily as we passed. I wheezed something in return, convinced it was an hallucination. At the summit Vin was waiting and I was glad to hear he'd also seen the children and that my sanity was intact!

The next big downhill dropped us through thick woods that blocked out the moonlight, the trees drooping, boughs laden with snow forcing us to duck as we ran. Again I pulled away from Vin, chuckling to myself as I heard the occasional 'thud', "ouch!"

The trail suddenly opened out onto a lane where the support car was in position. I stood with Mal and Andy, both drinking tea and eating cake, as we waited for Vin to finish his descent. He sprang into view with a shout of "Brilliaaaaant" and we were off again along the road to Fairholmes. This was the first real chance for us to open our stride and pick up some time and I had a struggle keeping up with Vin (and keeping him back with me!).

Round the North side of Ladybower and we were onto the last big climb up to Derwent Edge. The crew had radioed that a road was closed and they couldn't get to the last rendezvous but would instead meet us at the finish at the Ladybower Inn. We were on our own now and starting to feel tired. The climb up to the edge was very steep. Vin was somewhere in front again but I'm sure he could hear me panting. I was wheezing so hard it felt like I was trying to breathe through every orifice. I thought about getting my radio out so the support crew could hear as well but I was too exhausted to attempt it, and besides they would probably have thought I was having a violent asthma attack and called mountain rescue. At the top we set off together again along Derwent edge, another tricky, icy, rocky section with a few more painful falls.

The last mile and a half was downhill, partially icy, partially boggy and rocky. We were tiring and the batteries in the lights were starting to fade, and trips and falls became regular occurrences. Back to form, I flew off and kept turning round to check Vin was still on his feet. A hundred yards from the finish the guys were waiting with the camera to record our safe arrival. Thirteen steep slippery miles with 2500 feet of climbing completed, not as fast as we'd hoped (surprisingly it was the downhills that slowed us) but still respectably less than two hours.

Back at home we piled out of the car and finally managed to untie our shoelaces and throw the running clothes straight into the washing machine, then hit the shower. Within ten minutes back in the warmth and comfort the tiredness started to take over. Feeling a bit of a lightweight I announced that I was off to bed and left the other guys downstairs, still laughing about the evening's entertainment. Bed felt fantastic and sleep came quickly.

Getting a fix of energetic stupidity has a downside. Like a junkie you need another hit soon, and it has to be bigger, better and harder than the last one. It was only a couple of days after the run when the question "What next?" reared its head. What next indeed? We took a quantum leap into new (for us) territory!

oooOooo

Coast to Coast

Day 1. Tuesday 9ᵗʰ May 2006. St Bees Head to Rosthwaite.
25 miles

A full eighteen months of planning, preparation and training later we were standing on the beach at St Bees on the Cumbrian coast, feeling a shaky combination of nervousness and excitement. Vin was once again my running partner but there were changes to the rest of the team. Mal had switched from support crew to mountain biking athlete, and Andy was joined in the crew by Justin who would have been involved in the night fell run had he not gone to New Zealand for several months. The plan was an optimistic one - to run 180 miles across England, coast-to-coast, roughly following Wainwright's famous walking route over the Lake District, the Pennines and the North Yorkshire Moors to Robin Hood's Bay on the Yorkshire coast, in just seven consecutive days of running. That made an average of about 26 miles of fell running per day for a week, over some tough mountainous terrain. Particularly optimistic considering that when I first had the idea I'd never run more than fifteen miles in one go, never mind a marathon, and no more than 25 miles in a whole week. Cycling had traditionally been my sport of choice, mountain biking mainly, but it had been over fifteen years since I had ridden competitively. My sporting claim to fame was finishing sixth in the downhill in the British Mountain Biking championships in Dalby Forest in 1992 (definitely Z-list fame, more Eddie the Eagle than Eddy Merckx). Despite the difficulty of the task, recruiting the team had been little trouble. Vin and Andy, true to their nature, had both ruled themselves well and truly 'in' almost before I had finished describing the plan. Mal, slightly more cautious, declared he could never run that far but would be willing to have a bash at biking it. This was a good idea, adding a new dimension to the event – man verses bike. Justin proved a little harder to convince, and it took several weeks of emails to New Zealand before he conceded and allowed his name to be added to the team-sheet.

The 'coast-to-coast' has become one of Britain's, if not the world's, most popular long distance walks, and was originally devised by Alfred Wainwright (1907-1991), who was an enigmatic and obsessive character. Wainwright will always be known for his seven Pictorial Guides to the Lakeland Fells. These handwritten and hand-drawn works of art have given inspiration to fellwalkers for over forty years. He was born into poverty, the son of a stonemason, in the Lancashire town of Blackburn in 1907. At the age of 23 he was fortunate to holiday in the Lake District. It was love at first sight. He described his first Lakeland visit: "I was utterly enslaved by all I saw. Here were no huge factories, but mountains; no stagnant canals, but sparkling crystal-clear rivers; no cinder paths, but beckoning tracks that clamber through bracken and heather to the silent fastnesses of the hills. That week changed my life." He spent 13 years compiling the seven Pictorial Guides to the Lakeland Fells, walking the fells every weekend, with raincoat, map and camera. He'd write-up each weekend's walk in the weekday evenings, making fine intricate hand drawings. Such was his devotion and obsession he delivered on the thirteen-year plan exactly two weeks early. The first Pictorial Guide to the Lakeland Fells was published in 1955. AW (as he has more recently become known) wrote in its introduction: "This book is one man's way of expressing his devotion to Lakeland's friendly hills. It was conceived, and is born, after many years of inarticulate worshipping at their shrines. It is, in very truth, a love-letter." During 1970-1, Wainwright devised the Coast-to-Coast Walk from St Bees Head to Robin Hood's Bay. Not wanting to be prescriptive about an exact route he merely indicated his personal favoured footpaths, suggesting each coast-to-coaster make their own preferred choice of route. Many disciples, however, insist on following exactly the way the great man trod. There is a stone tablet set into the windowsill of a south window of St James Church, Buttermere, as a memorial to AW. The window looks out on his favourite place to walk, Haystacks, where at his wish his ashes were scattered.

Once again Andy fired up the car stereo and *Carmina Burana* blared out across the beach and into the morning sunshine. The weather couldn't have been better and we all gave off a pleasant aroma of sun cream as a calm Irish Sea benignly lapped over the pebbly shoreline. The anticipation over, we were heading inland whilst Justin and Andy fired away at the cameras and video. We had a preset game plan – start slowly and carefully, look after our injuries, and, if things went well, increase the effort after day four.

Training for the run had, on the whole, gone well, but for myself time to train had become severely limited. At the time the idea was conceived I had a busy nine-to-five job and was also undertaking a post-graduate university course. The coast-to-coast idea wasn't the only conception as my wife had become pregnant with our second child just over a year before the event was scheduled. Following my exams in June 2005 I was offered extra work by the university. This involved writing a study pack and becoming module leader for a course they planned to run. Packing all this work in alongside a family life with a three-year-old daughter and pregnant wife proved challenging, and I have to offer my gracious thanks to my wife, Andrea, for letting me go running at all. Kipling would have been proud, as I filled every unforgiving minute with sixty seconds worth of distance run.

Go running I did, as often and as far as possible. And that was the problem. I had no real training plan. My first efforts were to increase my running distance from half marathon to 25 miles or so at a time. This I did fairly quickly in the first few weeks of 2005, and on the whole found it a hugely enjoyable experience – mental relaxation away from the hectic work and home life. The bad winter weather didn't bother me. In fact I worked on the philosophy that I needed to toughen up to run 180 miles, and so I chose to run at times when the weather was at its worst. One particular fierce hailstorm left my forehead and face numb and stinging, but during a short break in the hail the sun appeared and several stunningly bright concentric rainbows shone vividly under leaden grey skies. It was fiercely beautiful.

The Easter weekend offered my first chance to run several days in succession as my daughter's grandparents (God bless them) were having her to stay. I was pleased to have notched up 52 miles on my feet over the four days. However I still had no appropriate training plan and was, with hindsight, risking injury.

Most weekends during the warmer summer months of 2005 I was to be found trail running in the Peak District. I'd load up my Camelbak with the weight I was expecting to carry on the coast-to-coast and run over difficult terrain for twenty-something miles, preferably during the hottest part of the day. Revision of my map reading and navigational skills also featured on these runs as we would be entirely dependent on finding our route across the country, preferably without troubling the mountain rescue services. My feet were starting to take a battering. I'd always been prone to blisters throughout my life and now I had several fine specimens on each foot. Toenails were also in danger of extinction as one by one they blackened and dropped off. Again I saw this as all part of the toughening up process, a necessary suffering to get me through the coast-to-coast. Andrea wasn't so sure, and definitely found my tattered feet quite unattractive. My legs were also taking some punishment. I had been thinking that some of the trails we'd encounter on the run might be overgrown with brambles and other thorny flora, and I needed to be prepared for such an eventuality. Heath land in a favoured running area not far from home provided an excellent training ground. The path I usually took wound its way in a tortuous route around clumps of nettles and numerous small gorse bushes. However my new plan was to run in a straight line from one end of the heath to the other, forging through whatever nature placed in my way. No nettle, thistle, gorse bush or cowpat stopped me (although I did concede defeat on the straight-line rule when the farmer introduced several young bullock onto the land, most of which seemed to be directly in my way, staring at me in a 'come-and-have-a-go-if-you-think-you're-hard-enough' manner). In the shower post-run my legs were often red and angry looking and were tingling from nettle stings, and I had to pluck out many tiny gorse thorns. But in a bizarre way it felt satisfying. The strategy brought me closer to nature. One fine evening as I ran onto the heath I caught site of two foxes playing energetically in the last warmth of the setting sun. They hadn't seen or heard me and hadn't smelt my hot sweaty scent as I approached from downwind. I quietly slowed to a halt and stood watching their game of play fighting. Two or three minutes passed before they sensed my presence and darted for cover into nearby woods.

On another occasion I was brought a little too close to nature. The particular run took me into the Chatsworth estate adjacent to the village of Baslow. I was heading straight down the hillside to the north of the main house, rapidly descending a bank that was densely covered in chest high thistles. Relaxed, moving swiftly and sure-footedly in the lazy afternoon sun, I was enjoying the view whilst confidently brushing any taller thistles away from my face. As far as unexpected moments go this was a massive one. Not six feet in front of me a huge brown mass exploded upwards. An antlered head and muscular body spun violently whilst four flailing limbs thrashing for grip on the steep surface. The deer was either sleeping or had seen me approaching and chose to hide in the undergrowth, hoping I'd pass by. Unwittingly I had run straight on top of it and at the last moment its survival instinct kicked in and it took flight. I'm not sure which of us was the most shocked. We all but pounded into each other before sprinting in opposite directions, hearts racing and adrenaline screaming through our startled bodies.

My first significant running injury occurred early one fresh Sunday morning as I made the tricky descent down Alport Dale. I was being careful on the steep uneven ground, or so I thought, when my left foot missed its placing and I went over badly on the ankle. This hurt and I swore, but was unable to stop straight away due to my momentum on the harsh gradient. After several hopping hobbling steps a soft grassy area appeared and I allowed myself to half fall, half roll to a halt. I was about 50 minutes into a three-and-a-half hour run. Common sense would have been to turn back but, conscious of my limited training time, I decided to rest for a minute or two and then see how it felt. It felt OK. Not right, but OK. Gingerly I continued down the mountain and was pleased to feel as though I was 'running it off'. A few minutes later on the relative flat of the Snake Pass valley I had no pain so I continued as planned. However, an hour and a half later the pain gradually returned, consistently increasing in intensity, and I still had an hour's running to get back to the car. If I placed my left foot on ground that sloped to the left there was no pain but a camber the other way forced me to wince and limp. For several days after I applied ice to my bruised ankle, wore elastic strapping, and rested. Despite these remedial efforts I was left with a permanent clicking sound on rotation of my foot.

oooOooo

A mile and a half of the coast-to-coast run and so far our ankles were holding up well as we turned off the road for the first small climb. Up through a few fields we caught our last views of St Bees and the Irish Sea. Mal had long gone. We'd watched him effortlessly speed away from us on the outskirts of the village, barely turning the pedals. With a hundred and eighty miles to go two wheels and a helmet suddenly seemed like a mighty fine idea. The footpath we'd taken brought us onto a small road heading due east and, just as we'd set foot on the tarmac, the support car appeared in front of us, approaching out of a shimmering dusty heat-haze, a little more 'Lawrence of Arabia' than 'Lads in the Lake District'. It was quite an hilarious sight as Andy was sitting on the passenger window ledge with only one leg in the car, broadcast TV camera on his shoulder, filming us whilst simultaneously waving a can of Red Bull. We had a few minutes light-hearted banter with the crew whilst running that section. They filmed us running from behind, and it was too tempting to avoid dropping the shorts and giving them a running 'moony'. Spirits were high and, whilst filming, Andy asked how we were feeling. Vin replied, "Not bad, we've only got about 175 miles to go" Instinctively Vin and I both shouted "Brilliaaaaant", and with that the crew car sped off to meet Mal at the first Rendezvous at Ennerdale Bridge.

The shout of 'Brilliant' had become Vin's trademark, frequently heard whenever any ludicrous challenge is suggested. At over six feet tall and weighing only eleven stones (that's 154 pounds, or 70 kilograms depending on your preferred units) he is the most athletic member of the team, partially a result of his having more time than the rest of us to go out and train, and partly due to an intrinsic ability to push himself to the point of vomiting every time he trains. He's also the youngest by nearly ten years and has an infectious enthusiasm for any outdoor activity, matched by an ability to eat his weight in food.

It wasn't long before we arrived at the first moderate climb of the run, up Nannycatch Lane adjacent to Dent Hill. Following Mad Dog's orders we geared down to a fast walk up the steep lane. The top came quickly and easily, and the lane switched to bridleway. The firm trail crossed the hillside before descending to a stream, and running this section was hugely enjoyable. This would have made for fantastic biking and we agreed to tell Mal what he'd missed by taking his route.

Once on the lanes two or three miles from the rendezvous point we decided to call on the radio to see if the crew were in position. Mal heard us clearly from his position climbing out of Ennerdale towards Great Borne, Floutern Cop and Buttermere but the corner of a hill blocked out the crew. A three way conversation ensued with Mal (who'd been through the rendezvous point) relaying our messages to the crew and theirs back to us.

We reached the checkpoint to find Andy and Justin, each holding a cup of tea, sunbathing in deck chairs in a gravel car park pleasantly situated in a small copse of trees on the west bank of Ennerdale Water. All they needed was a tartan blanket over their laps to give it the 'right' look. The recently boiled kettle sat on the portable gas stove next to the car, a thin wisp of steam drifting from its spout as if suggesting the impending arrival of *Aladdin's* Genie. The overriding ambience was one of calm relaxation, yet I was breathing heavily and sweating too much for comfort. The car boot was open and the insides resembled a delicatessen. A small refrigerator sat neatly in one corner. A thin wire trailed to it from the car's cigarette lighter to provide the power to keep the perishable foods cold. We all grazed on malt loaf and flapjack; Vin and I stretched our muscles in the shade and made the most of the short rest.

We were only eleven miles into the first day – a little early for a pit stop, but from here on we would be into the first real mountains and unreachable by the crew. The midday sun was quite fierce and we could tell from the map that there would be limited opportunity for shade for the rest of the day. For safety we chose to take one of the more powerful radios the crew had available. Camelbaks refilled, we set off for the south bank of Ennerdale Water, conscious that the crew would be filming us for some distance with their long lens camera gadgetry. Ennerdale Water is the most westerly of the lakes and probably the most remote, being the only one without a road alongside. Carved by a glacier it is 2.5 miles long 3/4 mile wide and 148 feet deep. The valley in which it lies still remains largely unspoilt, and there are moves by conservationists to keep it that way. A partnership called 'Wild Ennerdale' has been created with the aim: "To allow the evolution of Ennerdale as a wild valley for the benefit of people relying more on natural processes to shape its landscape and ecology."

The run alongside the lake was incredibly beautiful, and we stopped a couple of times to take some video and photographs of our own. Despite our careful running style over the loose rocky trail we made good progress and passed several small groups of walkers, some of whom we had a brief chat with, and some were also coast-to-coasters. The high fells of Pillar, Great Gable, Grey Knotts and Hay Stacks were looming ever closer, hanging threateningly over us but we were having too much fun to worry about what was coming ahead.

The first navigational error occurred during my watch as we ran past the trail we intended to take to cross over to the north side of the valley beyond the lake. However this proved beneficial, as we were able to continue on a wide shaded forest trail for a few more miles before crossing the River Liza further up the valley.

The track on the north side of the river up to Black Sail hut was also wide, and running would have been easy if it hadn't been for the gradual persistent incline, occasionally steep, and the easterly headwind. Curse that wind! One reason we chose to run from west to east was that the prevailing wind would be blowing from behind us, helping us along. And here it was, having done a full about-turn, being stubborn and difficult. Slipping into 'stubborn and difficult' mode ourselves we pressed on up the mountain. We could have run all this section but to do so with over a hundred and sixty miles to go would have been foolish. Instead we took regular short walk breaks on the steeper sections. I was glad of this as my energy levels were starting to flag; a short snack stop at Black Sail was pencilled in.

Three or four walkers were chatting when we reached Black Sail hut, a small stone built iconic youth hostel clinging to the mountainside at the head of the valley. As we arrived all but one of them left. We got talking to the guy remaining as we sat in the sun and ate our flapjack and energy bars. The view was stunning with high mountains standing over us on three sides, and the wild valley stretching back to the west. The guy's name was Pat and he was walking the coast-to-coast. We explained about our run and that we were raising money for charity, and he kindly donated a few pounds to the cause. He was also interested in my GPS wristwatch that we were using for time distance and pacing measurement. Pat had a hand-held GPS navigation device that he was using in preference to map and compass, having downloaded his route onto the device beforehand. Before we left him we also discovered that he was heading to Rosthwaite in Borrowdale, the same destination as ourselves.

Quarter of a mile past Black Sail our planned route took us north easterly up the very steep slope of Loft Beck. Over the millennia the beck had cut a narrow channel straight down the fall line of the mountain, and on the right hand side of the stream a crude path had evolved under the passage of thousands of pairs of boots. The gradient was severe and in places the path resembled a badly made staircase, loose stones and wiry grassy vegetation combined with occasional sudden turns provided great potential for bone-snapping stumbles. This, not surprisingly, was another walking section. We decided to climb the beck non-stop but monitor our breathing to ensure we weren't pushing too hard. Again the view from the top was superb and we couldn't resist the photo opportunity.

Just under the summit of Grey Knotts the last of the day's climbing was over and we set about carefully picking our footing down the long descent to the valley bottom. We had travelled over twenty miles and our joints were getting loose and unstable and one bad twist would likely mean the end of the event for which we had put in so much work.

We were heading almost due east down a dismantled quarry tramway, the surface of which was entirely loose broken slate. This was very difficult running, a conflict between keeping the speed and footing safe and not fighting gravity and overstressing the thigh muscles. We danced down like crazed ballerinas, occasionally loosening some of the slate and causing a mini-landslide. Directly in front and several hundred feet below we could see the road leading up Honister

Pass from Rosthwaite, and, as if transported there by our subconscious will, the crew car appeared around a bend in the road. I grabbed the radio from the webbing in Vin's backpack and called out to see if they could hear us. The sound of Mal's voice confirmed they could, and we arranged a team rendezvous at the mine buildings at the top of the pass, a mine that is England's only working slate mine, still extracting Westmorland Green slate.

Mal had successfully completed his day, although his coast-to-coast very nearly ended ignominiously as he apparently had a big slide on some gravel and nearly crashed within the first ten minutes.

There had been an entertaining meeting between the biker and support crew on the road from Buttermere to Honister Pass after Mal's descent from Floutern Cop. This was an unscheduled stop, Andy and Justin happening across him as he cycled up the pass. On being questioned about his enjoyment of the long downhill section Mal was evidently disappointed by the conditions of the trail, after he was required to get off and push his bike down some of the mountain, having pushed it up the other side. His description of the track was "Bastard boggy and bastard unrideable bridleway. It doesn't say that on the map!!"

Over the top of the pass he eventually raced, and beat, the crew car down to the Bed and Breakfast. This was pleasing for one sometimes considered the comparatively sensible member of the team, occasionally acting as our 'safety valve' to prevent stupidity becoming foolhardiness. That is not to say Mal doesn't partake in activities that the general population would consider extreme; scuba diving, rock climbing, ice climbing, snowboarding and heli-skiing featuring heavily in his 'activities' portfolio.

After the brief rendezvous Vin and I set off once again, down the road initially, accompanied by the crew car with Justin filming as we ran, before we cut off to the north and headed off road down another steep descent to the River Derwent, with another rendition of our 'ankle saving' dance as the terrain became steep rocky and loose. The river, when we reached it, looked inviting with shallow fast water flowing over rocks, shaded by overhanging tree branches. An old stone-built bridge gave the scene picture-postcard beauty. Another radio call to the crew followed and Mal and Justin wandered the 200 yards or so from the B+B to find Vin and me sitting with our legs submerged in the cooling water.

This had turned out to be one of the best day's running I had ever experienced; fantastic scenery, perfect weather, and challenging terrain. We'd covered 25 miles with 3000 feet of climbing and descent in four hours 25 minutes. But it had taken its toll on our ankles. We both had soreness at the point of our previous ankle injuries and Vin's was swollen. The following day we would both be into new territory never having run the day after a marathon. And we planned to run seven in a row!

The short stroll with Mal and Justin to the B+B was very pleasant but my legs felt a little stiff. Would they recover? Our accommodation in Rosthwaite (situated in a widening of the valley at the southern end of Borrowdale, named by the Norse and meaning "the clearing with the heap of stones") was owned by a lady called Rachel and was in keeping with the rest of the day - an immaculate white painted farmhouse standing proudly in the valley bottom. Rachel's perfectly manicured lawn and gardens sat in stark contrast to the rugged wild fells that towered over from all sides. The village has long been a popular spot with artists and authors and it was easy to see why. It was a favoured place of Wordsworth, and Beatrix Potter owned two farms in the surrounding area. Alfred Wainwright is quoted as saying, "A fellwalker based in Rosthwaite is like a king with many thrones", so varied are the walking and climbing possibilities in all directions. In a far corner of the garden stood a large cage in which perched a brightly coloured parrot that entertained us with its convincing mimicry of the whistles and commands that are used to control a sheep dog. A field opposite the front door contained a smattering of sheep. Whilst at that time they grazed quietly and appeared the epitome of docile calm they were to become our nocturnal nemeses.

We flopped down on Rachel's lawn and allowed ourselves to be fed and watered by Justin, who for interest sake was keeping account of what we all ate and drank during the event as there was an unofficial competition going on to see who could consume the most calories in the week. Drugged up on exercise-produced natural endorphins, drinking and lying in the sun, at that moment life was fantastic and the world was a great place to be. Andy was in the sitting room using the laptop computer, which had a problem. He had been kindly allowed to use the house telephone socket to get an Internet connection to try and fix it. After a good muscle stretch on the lawn the four of us headed inside to shower (and cold soak the legs for the athletes) and chill out for a couple of hours before evening meal. Rachel had to pop down the road to the local pub to work for a while. We were all quite surprised when she left us, five complete strangers, alone in her house. She gave us instructions to expect a walker to arrive and to show him to his room. Apparently his name was Pat!

The chill-out time became a constant grazing session as Vin, Mal and myself nibbled our way through tubs of dried fruit nuts and seeds, and drank our pre-made carbohydrate and protein drinks whilst we related the events of the day to each other. Andy and Justin sat on dining chairs around the large polished table, tinkering with the laptop, whilst the 'athletes' lay on the floor with legs raised on chairs to speed recovery. The telephone rang and we all looked at each other wondering whether to answer it. Mal stood up first, strode over, picked up the handset and gave a tentative "hello". It was a potential bed and breakfast customer, who was advised that the owner wasn't available, and told to ring back later. Within minutes a tired looking man in walking gear arrived at the front door asking for B+B. I asked if his name was Pat. He said not, and I had to apologetically tell him that the B+B was full. He had my sympathies as he hobbled slowly off down the road to seek out a bed for the night, clearly exhausted.

oooOooo

Rachel was obviously a busy woman. She had that tanned, weathered look of someone who had spent all her life among the mountains, as indeed she had. Born in the farmhouse next door, Rachel had lived in Rosthwaite all her life and clearly knew the local fells and people extremely well. We couldn't decide how old she was, our estimate varying between fifties and early seventies, but she was in very good shape and had, apparently, recently been to Everest Base Camp. Mal had to use her telephone to ring her to get her to return to her house as we were booked in the pub for a meal, and Pat had not yet arrived. She quickly returned on a bicycle, and we were just about to walk to the pub as the man Vin and I met at Black Sail strode into the garden. It was, of course, the same Pat, and we all greeted him heartily. Except for Rachel as she was a little put out by his late arrival. However, she soon mellowed under the spell of his mild demeanour.

The stroll to the pub in Stonethwaite was a slow one, but well worth it. Looking back to the west, high above Honister Pass, the setting sun had painted a few wispy thin high-altitude clouds a dramatic pastel pink and purple, whilst a cacophony of birdsong echoed from all directions through the sweet, clear evening air. Once in the pub a round of drinks was bought, a suitable table acquired in the corner, and food ordered from the impressive menu. Pat arrived and was invited to join us moments before the omnipresent Rachel leapt from the pub's kitchen and served our meals – some of the best lamb and vegetables on the planet.

The team briefing for the next day took place in the pub once we'd eaten. Day two looked ominously long with a huge amount of climbing and descending. The runners and Mal planned to follow the same route, which seemed sensible as all three would spend most of the day out of radio contact with the crew and there was only one likely refuelling stop at Patterdale.

The stroll back to the B+B was even slower than the one to the pub, and half way back Rachel whizzed past on her bike heading to unlock the house.

Sleep was generally restful that night, which is a little unusual for me following such a long run. Restful that is until four-o-clock in the morning when 'the devil's' sheep went for the world record at loud bleating; a volume such that we all thought it had broken into the house and was standing on our pillows. We wished we'd all had the lamb at the pub!

oooOooo

Jim Peters and Arthur Smith

Day 2. Wednesday 10th May 2006. Rosthwaite to Bampton.
26 miles

A full team practice day had been planned and executed just over a week before we set out on the coast-to-coast. We thought this necessary as for some of us our navigation was, at best, a little 'rusty', and for others finding their way out of bed in a morning was something of a challenge. We needed to be sure we wouldn't get ourselves lost, and more importantly that the support crew could be where we needed them at the right time and thus able actually to 'support'. This logistics test took place in the Peak District, in the region of Bakewell and Stanton Moor, and was on the whole a success. Everything was tested — individual navigation, the radios and other equipment, Justin's biking skills, and whether we could fit everything into the team car. Nobody got lost. Well, nearly! The crew took a minor, and I like to think deliberate (honestly!) diversion whilst transporting the runners to their drop off point. Vin and I watched in silence from the back seat of the car as Andy and Justin, deep in philosophical discussion and distracted by the aesthetic beauty of the lower end of Lathkill Dale, drove us speedily past the left turn we should have taken. On reaching the village of Youlgreave I hinted that a navigator's glance at the map might be in order. After a sudden halt followed by few moments of head scratching and map rotating from the front seats we were back on track. Other than that, everything worked, Andy had the kettle on when everybody else reached the rendezvous point, but no, the gear wouldn't all fit in the car. More significantly, during the run I went over badly on my right ankle twice in a short space of time, and it quickly swelled and turned a surprising and worryingly vivid shade of purple. This wasn't good.

A roof box was quickly borrowed to cure the storage issue (thanks to the Bedding brothers for that), and Mal helped by deciding that he probably didn't actually need to take four wheels and two frames with him after all. The crew proved they could do it and we athletes were left confident that we'd be well supported. A cure for the ankle, however, couldn't be quickly found and I spent the proceeding week resting it as much as possible, applying ice, strapping it in elasticated bandage and praying to the running Gods for leniency. I attempted a run three days later and managed a pitiful half a mile before having to stop due to the pain. At the eleventh-hour I'd made a pig's ear of my physical condition. I was as sick as a parrot, like a bear with a sore head, wore a face like a bulldog chewing a wasp, was as mad as a bottle of fish; a whole menagerie of bad-tempered grumpiness. After training and preparing for over a year the potential prospect of not running the event due to a last minute injury was, to say the least, a major psychological blow.

oooOooo

But running the event I certainly was, and during breakfast on Day 2 the ankle problems were overshadowed by the enormity of the task ahead. The distance was up to 30 miles, with three huge ridges to cross before a long, steady, thigh-burning descent to the village of Bampton on the eastern edge of the Lake District. Conversation at the table swung between the themes of "kill that bloody noisy sheep" and "bloody hell, it could be hard today". Rachel breezed in and informed us that it would be hot and sunny again with no shade all day, then proceeded to try and tell Mal of another half dozen or so routes that he "should take" that would be easier than the one he'd planned. All of them sounded completely unrideable (but as it turned out that was mostly the case on the chosen route anyway!). Mal was slightly upset that his wish for cool overcast weather had been trumped by my wish for more hot and sunny. My wish was now looking foolish.

Pat was sounding chipper and was looking forward to his short days walk to Grasmere, and it was reassuring to listen to his supportive comments and confidence that we could actually get all the way to Robin Hood's Bay on schedule.

Getting changed and prepared seemed to take longer than normal following breakfast, partly due to some nervous trepidation and partly the result of taking extra time to get smothered in sun cream as well as the usual Vaseline. Anyone who has done any long distance running will be all too aware of the effects of chafing, which can be unpleasant to say the least. On occasions it isn't felt during the run itself, but when the runner steps into the shower to clean down post-run he or she suddenly discovers the ability to yodel and dance like a hyperactive on speed as the water stings the sore spots. And why is it always the more intimate regions that suffer most? A good bit of chafing on the knees or shoulders could be displayed in a machismo demonstration of ones athletic prowess. An action man-like scar to the cheek that only appears on successful completion of a marathon would be a blemish worthy of pride and exaggerated discussion over far too many pints. But sore bleeding nipples and chafing in the groin are invariably ailments of a covert nature, their presence only likely to be betrayed by the occasional quiet whimper and pained facial tick. Any attempt by the sufferer of such delights to show them off in the pub would almost certainly result in further injury, this time of a non-accidental kind.

Vin's skin must be like leather as he used very little Vaseline but I was getting down my tub quickly smearing it everywhere that moved – armpits, feet, inner thighs, groin, and lower back and shoulders where my backpack contacted. Added to that I also sported a pair of highly fashionable nipple guards – like a polo-shaped plaster – that prevent bleeding nipples caused by the running vest constantly rubbing up and down.

Other preventative measures I was taking included high doses of multivitamins to keep my immune system buoyant and cod-liver oil and glucosamine supplements for joint care.

Stepping outside the house the strength of the sun hit us, even at nine-o-clock in the morning. No shade for several hours! I double-checked my Camelbak to ensure it was full of sports drink, and downed the rest of my carbohydrate 'pre-run' drink I'd made and started the evening before. We paid Rachel (who kindly knocked five pounds off the bill to give to the charity), said farewell and good luck to Pat, then *Carmina Burana* blared from the car and once again we were off with Mal in front of myself and Vin. Andy stood in the road recording the moment on his big camera.

The first half-mile was flat and on tarmac, and this was a good opportunity to assess how our legs felt the day following a fell marathon. Spirits and confidence were high as neither of us felt we had any cause to worry, legs coping well. Immediately after the small village of Rosthwaite we took a right turn up the first bridleway on the climb to Watendlath, and quickly caught Mal who was pushing his bike up the steep gradient. This was to become a recurring theme. The plan was for another steady day so we took the opportunity to stand for a few minutes and film the intrepid cyclist's struggles using my small video camera. Our pace here was faster than his so Vin and I headed onward knowing we'd all regroup later. The view behind us back into Borrowdale was as beautiful as you'd see anywhere, even with the slight haze from the hot weather.

Mal was clearly taking a steady start as well as he still hadn't caught us by the bottom of the short descent to Watendlath tarn, a descent punctuated by Vin's requirement to jump over a wall and scuttle off to an unseen place to answer the call of nature. In actual fact nature was not just calling on Vin, she was in an impatient mood and threatened to huff and puff and blow his house down. 'What goes up must come down' applied to our running on the mountains, but as far as Vin's bowels were concerned 'up' and 'down' needed replacing with 'in' and 'out'. And as a matter of urgency! Several minutes passed before he returned, hopping over the dry-stone wall and looking less fraught than the outward hop. After a slight adjustment to his running garments it was only a short jog to the tarn, with time to sit and relax for a moment and watch Mal bounce his way down the rocky trail. Even riding his full-suspension Specialized machine that was designed and built for this kind of terrain he looked to be taking a bit of an early morning pounding. There simply was no smooth line for him to ride, and when he reached us at the bottom I half expected to see his eyes, cartoon-like, rolling and shaking in their sockets. Alas, there was just the wide mouthed grin of a man enjoying himself.

This was the first rendezvous point of the day, too close to the start to be a refuelling stop but far enough for everyone to assess how they were coping on day two. More importantly it is the location of arguably the most scenic café in England, and worth the gamble for the crew that it would be open so early in the morning.

It wasn't!

But the crew still enjoyed the aesthetic beauty, and fired off numerous photos of the little hamlet and tarn, which sit 847 feet above sea level and are surrounded by fells in a classic 'hanging valley'. Meanwhile the athletes got stuck into the next climb up towards Blea Tarn. Again this was heavy going and a bike-push for Mal. The heat was getting fierce and he appeared to be generating his own personal weather system that rained constantly from his every pore. Once again we left him behind as we picked our way up the tussock grassy slope to the tarn. Another stop for some pictures near the tarn was used as an excuse to cool down a little and enjoy the spectacular view, a tactic repeated at the summit looking down the steep descent towards Thirlmere. Despite this being northern England there was a mirage-inducing heat shimmer over the near horizon, which gave the water in Blea tarn a swaying mystical appearance as if it was the back of a huge living beast slowly awaking from a deep slumber.

A quick radio call to Mal from this point told us he was still OK behind, and we were to head on down rather than wait for him. It started as a tricky descent as the grass was wet, uneven and slippery, and the gradient steep. I attempted to film as we ran but this turned out to be a ludicrous idea, as I needed all my concentration to stay on my feet and not twist an ankle. Vin took a couple of sliding falls as the tread on his shoes filled up with mud. After a quarter of a mile or so of reckless high-speed hobbling, slipping and sliding we reached a wall with a stile over it next to a stream. Vin stopped to clean the map case as he'd slid on it and there were brown mud stains preventing our reading the map. The mountain stream looked sparklingly clear and very inviting so I cooled off by dipping my cap in it and draping it straight back over my head. Trickles of cold water ran down the back of my neck and dripped off the peak onto my face and chest, and even in that heat it gave me goose bumps and made me shiver.

Over the stile the trail disappeared into a mass of trees, some recently fallen, others growing obliquely in foul-smelling swampy ground, all covered in thick moss and doing their best to impede our progress. The pace dropped to a walk as we climbed, jumped and slipped our way over the boughs and branches and slopped through the stinking mire. It was as if we'd stepped into Louisiana swampland, and we felt like extras in the film Southern Comfort. With a bit of imagination I could almost hear Ry Cooder's guitar twanging hauntingly, and half expected a crazed Creole woodsman to leap from the trees and attack us. Not surprisingly one didn't! Within 200 yards the terrain opened up into a wide and sunny forest track heading straight down the mountain, and we were running again, shafts of bright light piercing the canopy of far more healthy deciduous woodland. But not for long! Immediately after Harrop Tarn the gradient steepened and we were trying to run down narrow rocky gullies that twisted and wound between thick gorse bushes, interspersed with near vertical scrambles down slippery outcrops of rock. It was often only possible to see the track for six feet or so in front of us. Vin's cautious approach to descents was getting the better of him again and several times I got a hundred yards or so in front before stopping to check he was still following uninjured. This was Mal's planned route and I found myself cruelly laughing out loud at the prospect of him having to drag his bike down this unrideable trail after having dragged it all the way to the summit of the previous mountain. The map clearly indicated this was a bridleway, but, with the exception of Pegasus, I couldn't imagine a horse that could ever have got up it.

A hundred yards from the road at the side of Thirlmere we stopped to radio Mal to warn him of the trail conditions. We were more than a little surprised to hear him say that he was doing fine, riding along a lane near the Lake. As he was speaking Vin pointed over my shoulder and shouted, "He's there". I spun round and sure enough Mal was zipping along the road behind us, riding one handed, the other clutching his radio to his face.

"We're behind you," I shouted into the mike in true pantomime fashion. Mal turned, stopped his bike, and we all grouped together at the roadside, Vin and I amazed that he'd managed to beat us down. Mal explained that he'd met two walkers by the stile, who told him about the trail below and advised an alternative route that was further in distance and involved a little uphill, but was entirely on good rideable track. Wisely he had taken their advice and had a very enjoyable high speed ride down through the forest to the side of the lake, reaching it a few hundred yards to the north of our trail.

After relating to each other our stories of the first mountain of the day we bade farewell to Mal. He shot ahead along the road and we toddled along behind, all three of us heading for the bridleway up Raise Beck to Grizedale Tarn, which would be the second high point of the day. Raise Beck is another bridleway probably impassable to a horse; steep, rocky, loose and poker-straight up the mountain. Missed footing could result in a nasty fall over sharp rocks into the fast-flowing stream that plummeted down the narrow gorge. At the bottom of the climb we had to cross the stream, leaping from giant boulder to giant wobbly boulder, then scale a wall to reach the start of the bridleway. The river crossing provided another opportunity to soak my hat, and again this was spine-tingling, goose-bump refreshing. Vin and I adopted the same tactic that had been successful for the climb up Loft Beck the day before – steady climbing without getting short of breath, and no stopping. Three quarters of the way up, craning our necks up towards the towering skyline, we could see ahead the outline of someone with a bike on their shoulder struggling on all fours up a difficult section of trail. This could only be Mal. Sure enough we quickly caught him up and were again impressed by the quantity of 'rain' he was producing from his head down his chest and back. Dragging the bike up this mountain was clearly hard work, but he was doing exceptionally well and displayed no signs of stopping. He kindly stepped to one side to let us pass, and we agreed to re-group next to the tarn for some hard earned refreshment.

We had made ourselves comfortable sitting by the tarn for only a couple of minutes before Mal arrived, and we all tucked into pieces of flapjack that Justin had bought from Doncaster railway station a few days before. This particular flapjack had been chosen purely on the merits of its high calorific content – 600 kcal per piece. Not for slimmers! In fact not for healthy eaters at all as listed second in the ingredients was hydrogenated vegetable oil, a form of man-made super-saturated fat! But it was easy to eat and as fuel for long distance running it did the trick. We all commented that our packs were starting to feel light, which meant that we were all getting low on drink. Not to worry though, we were due to rendezvous with the crew about four miles away at the bottom of the next descent in Patterdale. We could refill the Camelbaks and get more food then. For a few moments we sat together, gazing over the tarn at the group of slowly moving dots that were walkers on top of the distant St Sunday Crag.

Not wanting to sit too long in the hot sun, which was by now very high in the sky, we were soon away, although Mal opted for a slightly longer and probably more deserved rest. After picking our way round the uneven marshy ground by the tarn we were off down the valley of Grizedale Forest on another rocky bridleway. Again sections were steep and loose, and the running pace was variable as we looked after our ankles. We expected Mal to pass us any moment on the descent but he must also have been riding with caution as we were still in front near the valley bottom where the trail opened into a wide gravel track. We had drunk all our fluid and our legs were starting to feel a bit wobbly as we ran down the uncomfortably steep tarmac lane into Patterdale, turning right at the main road to the rendezvous grid reference. Mal shot up to us from behind, announcing his arrival with a cheery "Hello". Keen to ensure the crew were in position I grabbed Vin's radio from the webbing on the back of his pack, held in the 'call' button and asked "Andy, J, are you there?" We were only half a mile or so from the checkpoint so well within radio range.

No answer!

Again "Andy, J, coneheads, are you there?" (Mal nicknamed the crew 'coneheads' as reference to their techno-babble conversations about the computer or cameras, which were completely unintelligible to we three athletes).

No answer again!

Slight concern was creeping in.

Mal rode on ahead. Two minutes later he called us on the radio: "There's no sign of the crew."

No crew! How could this be? We were two thirds of the way through the hardest day, in the mid-day heat, out of water and food with miles to go and another big climb in front of us, and our team had stood us up.

"But there is a shop," came another message from Mal.

A lifeline. Round a corner to the right there was indeed a small village store, Mal's bike leaning untidily up against its wall. Vin had no money. I checked my pack and managed to trawl out three pound coins. That won't get us much, we thought, and we made a note to take some sensible money with us the following day. If we made it that far!

Inside the store we found Mal clutching some sandwiches, a packet of crisps, a sizeable piece of cake, a large bottle of water and, more importantly, a spare ten-pound note. The latter we commandeered and engaged in what looked like a crazed trolley dash, grabbing food and water as quickly as we could. The three of us sat on the steps outside the shop, eating our newly acquired sustenance and grumbling at the apparent demise of our usually reliable support team. We bandied theories about.

Had they got lost? Possibly!

Had they crashed the car? Also a possibility!

Were they in a pub? Probably!

Alien abduction? Hmmm!

Had they got fed up and gone to a lap-dancing bar? Fortunately we knew of no such bar in the vicinity. Just as we had eaten all we could afford to buy, a red estate car sporting a roof box and mountain bike, and with 'Respect The Stupidity' emblazoned across the back window appeared at high speed from round the corner and was thrown to a halt. We were saved. Justin climbed out of the driving seat, and sensing our concern at the thought of having been abandoned, explained that he'd just had to leave Andy in a computer shop in Keswick and drive at break-neck speed to get to the rendezvous. The laptop had been badly infected and required several hours of specialist T.L.C. to put right. More relieved than annoyed, the three of us followed the car into a nearby parking area. Justin opened the boot, put the kettle on and buttered some malt loaf. We'd now been out in the sun for five hours or so, and the small area of shade under a tree at the rear of the car park was hugely welcome. A few cans of Red Bull were downed, and a route check showed the runners and rider going separate ways for the first part of the next leg. Mal had a flat road section to Brothers Water before the biggest climb of the whole coast-to-coast up Hayeswater Gill to The Knott and Kidsty Pike. Vin and I would take the longer but steadier climb up past Angle Tarn and then on to The Knott.

Feeling replete and more relaxed, we bode farewell to Justin and set off again. He was off back to Keswick to see how Andy and the laptop were getting on. This nearly turned into a long journey for him as he typed 'Keswick' into the satellite navigation system but failed to notice he'd accepted a route to Keswick in Kent (or somewhere down that way). His mistake soon became apparent though as Natalie (the voice of the sat-nav system) informed him he'd be there in four and a half hours.

oooOooo

It seemed to be getting hotter and hotter on the first ascent towards Angle Tarn, and Vin was looking longingly at my hat. Foolishly he'd not bothered to pack a hat to run in, and even decided to leave his Oakley sunglasses at home (crazy fool!). I generously offered a timeshare on my headgear, which he accepted without hesitation, almost snatched it out of my hand, dunked it in the nearest stream and plonked it on his head.

The climb up to Angle Tarn was unremarkable, apart from my mobile phone beeping away in a crazed fashion from somewhere deep in my Camelbak. Evidently we had just entered an area of mobile phone reception for the first time since Ennerdale Water, and half a dozen or so text messages suddenly flew in from the family and well-wishers wanting to know how we were getting on. Sending a couple of replies was another good excuse for a quick break. Over the brow at Satura Crag we had a fabulously clear view up to The Knott, and also down to Hayeswater, and below that the valley bottom. The magnitude of the climb became apparent looking at the cars travelling along the road from Kirkstone Pass as they appeared tiny, similar to the view one gets from an aircraft just after take off before it plunges into the clouds.

A fairly level section, half rocky outcrop and half narrow soft trail, led to the steeper slopes of The Knott, and we made regular calls on the radio in an attempt to contact Mal, certain that he would be on the hill above. As we started the steeper part of the climb a fit looking runner in red fell-running kit bounded sure-footedly and at very high speed down towards us. As he flew past he shouted a cheery "hello" and we were surprised to see he must have been well over 60 years old. It was evident that had we been racing him he would have left us trailing in his wake. "Still," we thought, "we've got a good twenty years training (or in Vin's case thirty) to get that good!" It was impressive.

Ten minutes into the steeper climb we caught site of Mal, again hauling his bike up unsuitable terrain. We quickly caught him and all stopped for a brief chat. He'd not heard us on the radio as his unit had somehow switched itself off. He was very pleased to see us as he required assistance of an unusual nature, asking us "Give me a song to sing, one that I like."

"Pardon?" we both replied.

"Give me a song to sing. I've bloody well got 'High on a hill stood a lonely goat-herd' from *The Sound of Music* lodged in a loop going round and round in my head. It's driving me nuts. I need something sensible to replace it."

We threw a few options his way and he settled on *American Pie*.

He'd also seen the old guy running, describing how he'd run past him up the hill at a speed that sounded not much slower than that of his descent. Mal also had some extra money in his pack, courtesy of two men, Rob and Allan, who'd questioned him about the foolishness of dragging a bike up The Knott. Apparently they'd "Never seen bikes up here before". Surprising that! After he told them what we were doing and the charity aspect, they kindly donated to the cause.

Vin and I continued ahead once more. Only now I found that *The Sound of Music* was highly contagious and that I was the one afflicted with the annoyance of singing 'High on a hill stood a lonely goat-herd'. Vin didn't help as he joined in with the 'Yodel-ay-he yodel-ay-he yodel-ay-he-hoo' parts. Evidently Mal and I had fallen into the same Von Trapp! The song simply would not leave my tortured brain. How do you solve a problem like Maria?

Round the top of The Knott we regrouped again at the highest point of the journey, the summit of Kidsty Pike. This point is widely considered to offer the best view throughout the coast-to-coast, and I wouldn't argue. Behind us we could see the vast expanse of the Lake District mountains stretching far into the haze, and it was exciting to think that we'd run and biked from over the far horizon in just two days. In front of us the terrain altered dramatically and we had our first view of the flatter lands heading east before the rising of the Pennines. This would be tomorrow's adventure, but first we had to descend from the peak and still run six miles or so to the village of Bampton near the head of Haweswater. Fans of the cult film *Withnail and I* will no doubt be aware that it was filmed in the area of Bampton. While we were all three together at the summit of Kidsty Pike we asked a rambler, sat sunning himself, to take our photograph with the Lake District fells in the background.

We had a choice of routes down to our destination – a steep thigh-burning descent down Kidsty Howes then a long flattish five miles along Haweswater, or stay high along High Raise followed by a more steady descent down Bampton Common. The fine weather and tired legs meant the steep descent was quickly dismissed and we set off with Mal in a north-north-easterly direction along the firm grassy ridge. On the first of the descents before the Common I noticed I had started with some knee pain, just on the lower outside edge of my left kneecap. It was enough to make me limp slightly but didn't stop me running. I was slightly concerned about this, but at the same time blissfully unaware of the devastating effects it would later cause.

On the map we had seen the possibility of cutting a short corner between two small paths at High Kop. This would require a bit more navigational skill, stopping at an exact location and taking a compass bearing across a level featureless section of the spur along which we were running. After taking care to ensure we didn't overshoot the correct point we took the compass reading from the map. It was easy enough, 90-degrees, due east! Rotating the instrument to point its arrow in our desired direction of travel we looked on the ground and it was evident that there was a well-worn path heading exactly where we wished to go. Clearly many other walkers had previously had exactly the same idea. Disappointed at not having to test some of our finer navigating skills we started along the path only to stop straight away as Vin's bowels heard another loud 'knock knock'. It was Nature again, calling back on her way home from a busy day at the office. Still in no mood for intestinal fortitude, she threatened him with imminent eruption of Vesuvius proportions. This time there was no cover, no walls to jump, nowhere to hide, just a large expanse of flat level grassy moorland. All in all a very poor choice of location for covert toilet operations! Frantically he hobbled and hopped away from the path, zigging and zagging before eventually stumbling upon a small hollow that was used by sheep to lay and shelter from the elements. Crouching and dipping his head down he was thankfully sufficiently out of sight for decency sake. This was becoming a worrying habit, and I became concerned he may have a contagious illness and that I'd also soon be scurrying for the undergrowth before exploding like a

Roman candle. But then perhaps Vin simply liked his toileting to be pleasantly scented with the aroma of Lake District fells. At his current rate of alfresco evacuation it was likely that the Lake District fells would soon become unpleasantly scented with the aroma of Vin's toileting. Looking away and trying not to think of what he was using in the absence of toilet paper (maybe there was still a sheep or two in the little hollow!) I filled the time and distracted my mind by videoing Mal as he swiftly rode down the spur behind us.

The run down Bampton Common was relatively fast; averaging around eight minutes per mile, and for the first time ever I sensed Vin was starting to struggle. We'd been running for nearly six hours and I could no longer hear his footsteps close behind me. A quick glance back confirmed that he had indeed dropped a little way behind. I was feeling quite good and being ahead was a new experience to me. So many times he'd stretched me to my limits in an attempt to keep up with him, so I decided to have a little fun and win a small battle myself. I kept the pace up. But not for long! After about a mile and a half common sense prevailed as I remembered we still had 120 miles to run, and slowed to let him catch up. I was feeling the strain in my legs and told Vin I was getting a little tired. He was glad to hear it, saying he had just about had enough for the day but daren't admit it until I'd said it first! I took this as a moral victory, never having beaten him before.

The last mile into Bampton was very steep downhill and we were struggling, thighs burning, knee stinging with every step, and loose ligaments in all our joints making them unstable on the uneven terrain. Great care had to be taken to avoid a bad fall or twist. Vin attempted a long jump over a short boggy section, but his strength had expired. Amusingly for me there was very little jump, and what jump there was certainly wasn't long. I walked round the swamp, watched and laughed, entertained as he struggled to extract himself from the putrid foul-smelling knee-deep quagmire. As we reached tarmac for the finish into the village the day's efforts were clear as we both started wobbling and bumping uncontrollably into each other. We were bonking!

I feel the need to explain.

Far from being a term for activities relating to any kind of sexual gratification, in this context bonking is invariably a wholly unpleasant affair. When the body's energy stores become excessively depleted due to prolonged intense exercise the muscles become extremely tired and blood sugar levels crash, with some alarming effects. Fine motor control can disappear (hence the wobbles) and summoning up strength enough to give a weak kitten a fair fight requires surprising mental determination, a determination that can unfortunately evaporate along with other desirable cerebral functions such as logic, concentration and an even temper. In the absence of urgent sugary sustenance really bad cases require, and produce, a good dose of delirium to ease the suffering. We had both turned into the bunnies that weren't powered by Duracell. Despite our efforts to keep piling in the calories during the day we had failed to prevent 'the bonk'. Fortunately as far as bonks go this wasn't a bad one (I could write a book entitled 'My best and worst bonks' but thankfully I won't). We were nearly home and dry for the day, and knowing this made it bizarrely enjoyable as we lumbered down into Bampton, giggling and careering around like a brace of drunken idiots. Mal appeared from a trail to our left and had a laugh at our expense as we struggled erratically trying to maintain a straight course down the lane, describing what he saw as a double 'Jim Peters moment'. Jim Peters was a fine international marathon runner, setting world record times on several occasions. Unfortunately he is best remembered for a race he failed to finish. The 1954 Commonwealth Games marathon was held in Vancouver in oppressively hot conditions. Peters set out at near world record pace and entered the stadium with a seventeen-minute lead and only a few hundred metres to go. Suffering badly from heatstroke and dehydration he wobbled and swayed along the track, staggering towards the finish. He fell several times before finally collapsing just short of the finish line, whereupon he was rushed to hospital. This was arguably the biggest, most famous and, unfortunately for Jim, the most public bonk ever. He retired from athletics following that race.

The bed and breakfast was very close. Mal got there before us and gave us accurate directions over the radio, which was useful as we were losing the ability to think for ourselves. Justin was waiting with the crew car boot open, ready for our urgent feed. On turning a right hand bend we could see the two of them just over a small hump-backed bridge that crossed a stream. Although rising only four or five feet or so, getting over that bridge mid-bonk felt as if we were dragging an anvil tied to each leg. We both hobbled over to the car, half collapsed on a picnic table, and began a crazed feeding frenzy that had Justin both amazed and in stitches. Noting everything we ate, for the next ten minutes Justin was very busy with his pen and paper. My blood sugar must have been very low as the first thing I wanted was jelly; cubes of jelly, straight from the block. I ate a whole block in a minute or two, and it was divine. This was washed down with huge gulps from my ready-made carbohydrate and protein drink. Next came several pieces of cake and buttered malt loaf, then a huge bowl of muesli with plenty of milk, and numerous handfuls of mixed nuts and fruit we'd nicknamed 'scrummy'. Vin was digging his way through bagels and cake before joining me with muesli. We were gavaging and guzzling food down our gullets faster than force-fed foie-gras geese. Halfway through the feast Andy poked his head out of a first floor window just above us and shouted an enthusiastic "Wey-heyyy". He'd been in his room yet again attempting to upload the website using his mobile phone but could only get a sketchy signal if he perched on the windowsill and dangled half out of the window. Still, it was an improvement but was apparently very slow.

Andy was in his element – happiest when tinkering with technology. The nickname of Bondy had been coined many years previous due to his James Bond-like ability to produce a gadget to assist (or sometimes complicate) any situation. His enthusiasm for adventure matches that of the rest of us, although he'd admit that his role was usually one of technological expert and all round support guy, and as far away from physical exertion as possible. Although usually a mostly nocturnal creature he had so far been performing remarkably well in dragging himself out of bed each morning.

My wrist-mounted GPS device told us we'd run 26 miles in six hours and two minutes. Not usually a good time for a marathon, but we had climbed and descended nearly 8,000 feet over very rough terrain. After a brief sit in the shade we carried our bags into the pub and headed for the showers to get cleaned up and give our legs a cold soak. Andy decided enough was enough on the hanging out of the window aspect, packed his laptop and phone into the car and drove up the nearest hill to get a better signal.

A good stretch and rest was definitely in order. After popping a small foot blister and painting on 'New Skin' I lay on my bed, feet raised on the pillows whilst Justin, my room mate for the night, chatted with Vin and Mal. All our rooms opened out onto a landing, and with the room doors open we could all chat together. Mal and Vin shared a twin room whilst Andy, the snorer, was in solitary confinement so as not to disturb the athletes' sleep. The early evening sun was still warm but with the room windows open a very pleasant cooling breeze blew through, and we all started to feel relaxed and human again. Vin, however, was taking some kind of non-human form on the landing as he performed his bizarre stretching routine, contorting himself into forms usually the reserve of plasticine models and circus acrobats. I couldn't watch, it looked too painful, preferring instead to doze to some music on my MP3 player.

A radio call to Andy told him to return as we had a table booked for evening meal. Just before we walked downstairs to the pub I had a pleasant surprise. My mobile phone beeped into life as my parents sent a text message saying they were on their way to visit us. They were staying in Keswick to see the jazz festival and had decided on the quick trip over to Bampton to give us some support. The sudden improvement in mobile phone signal provided the opportunity for a welcome and emotional phone call to Andrea and Hannah.

I was the first into the pub dining area and, as I stood perusing the menu, a slightly abrasive southern accent addressed me with the line "You're one of those crazy runners then are you"? He sounded familiar. I turned to the next table to see the TV entertainer Arthur Smith sitting with another man, finishing off the most fantastic looking piece of chocolate cake. We got chatting as the rest of the team ambled over to our table. He too was coast-to-coasting having walked that day from Patterdale, and like many people we met en-route thought we were slightly crazy. Most unlike his persona from the 'Grumpy Old Men' series he appeared extremely pleasant and interested in our jaunt.

Just as we were ordering our food my parents arrived. I was really pleased they were able to see us midway through the event, they being responsible for shaping me into the mountain-loving outdoors type that I am. In my youth both parents were heavily involved with the scouting movement, to which I was naturally introduced. My particular troop wasn't the sit-around-tying-knots type (if any actually are) but more into building bridges from ropes and telegraph poles, zip-lines down hillsides, natural shelters to sleep in or rafts to race around muddy lakes. I'd often come home resembling *The Creature from the Black Lagoon*. My mother, June, didn't seem to mind so long as I got hosed down and stripped off outside the house before heading for the bath. My father, Geoff, walked the coast-to-coast solo just a few years ago. Two years ago my mother had a fall and required an emergency hip replacement. Within a year of the operation they sent the surgeon a photograph of her standing on top of a mountain in Sardinia – a mountain she had just walked up. Both still mountain-walk, all over the world, and have transmitted to me the enormous value of being in the hills, and also of taking the occasional calculated risk. This was my breeding stock, of which I am naturally proud.

After a round of greetings and introductions (my parents had not previously met Vin) they chatted briefly to Arthur Smith and took place at his table as he left with his fellow walker.

Once again the food was excellent and we ate until we were uncomfortably full then headed to bed for another early, yet disturbed night.

oooOooo

Bulls and Parrots

Day 3. Thursday 11th May 2006. Bampton to Kirkby Stephen.
22 miles

It started around four o'clock in the morning. The demons that were attempting to sabotage our sleep had caught a flock of wild birds and put them in our rooms to sit on the bed heads and sing as loud as they could for three hours. Or so it seemed. Once again the wildlife had dragged us kicking and screaming from our slumbers. Concerned that I'd not had enough sleep I lay in bed awake at seven o'clock and took my pulse rate (a higher than normal heart rate would indicate my body was still trying to recover from the previous days exertions). Recently my early morning pulse rate had been around 38 to 40 beats per minute, and I was pleasantly surprised, and also relieved, to find that this morning it was only 42. These are low figures indicating that I was very fit, as one would expect with the quality and duration of my training program. Extreme athletic events such as the one we were embarked upon could potentially pose a risk of significant medical problems, especially if there was an underlying silent abnormality. For this reason I had allowed myself to be persuaded by Andrea to visit my GP for a check-over ten months before the start of the coast-to-coast. The health check started well, heartbeat low and regular (as expected), chest sounds clear (no surprise), but my doctor raised an eyebrow when she took my blood pressure. She paused for a few seconds then took it again. Another pause.

"We'll just get you to lie on this couch for five minutes, then take it again" she said. "Your blood pressure is a little high. This may be because you've just had your jabs." (Immediately before entering the doctor's office my family had received a few holiday vaccinations as we were soon to travel to New Zealand, Bali and Singapore) "so we'll see if it comes down". It didn't. Behind the GP my wife was smirking with an expression that was half "I told you so" and half "this is really funny".

I was immediately booked for some tests – an ECG to check the electrical activity in my heart, and a series of blood tests for liver and kidney function and cholesterol levels.

After a couple of trips to the hospital I was back to my GP for the results. The blood tests were all normal but my ECG was a little unusual. "Great," I thought sarcastically. "She's going to tell me I can't run." The doctor explained that the abnormality may be physiological rather than pathological – my hearts 'normal' response to a high level of training. To be on the safe side I was referred to a cardiologist for an ultrasound examination of my heart and also to have a 24-hour blood pressure monitor fitted. I went home to wait for the appointments and told Andrea, who this time didn't laugh but adopted a more worried expression.

The day before the echocardiogram appointment I ran a 26 mile trail run in the Peak District partly for training and partly to check out the route for an upcoming event (The Chatsworth Challenge). This was indeed a challenging run, taking four-and-a-quarter very hot hours, and I considered it useful to have done this prior to the scan. I was scanned by the consultant himself who is also a keen road and fell runner. He was interested to hear about the coast-to-coast plans and also about my previous day's run. As soon as he started the scan he was able to reassure me, saying that my heart was finding it all too easy just lying on the bed, that it looked an 'athletic' heart and also that the ECG anomaly was simply a result of my physical conditioning. I was still to have the 24-hour blood pressure monitor though. This involved wearing an inflatable cuff around my upper arm, connected to a walkman-sized machine worn on a belt around my waist. The machine pumped the cuff up every half hour through the day and hourly throughout the night, repeating the process five minutes later if I moved during the reading. This was not conducive to a good night's sleep and I looked exhausted and bleary-eyed the following day when I returned to have the device removed.

A week or so later I received a letter from the cardiologist. The results were all normal. I didn't have high blood pressure. The abnormal results at the GP were due to 'white coat hypertension' – increased blood pressure caused by the nervousness of having the readings taken, or in my case trying too hard to relax and make the readings normal.

All the results were normal. I was fit to run, and was happy, but more importantly Andrea was happy. I had the 'green light' to continue training and reset my sights on the coast-to-coast.

oooOooo

We'd all been woken by the birdsong. Even Andy, who can usually sleep through the water-buffalo-mating, nasal-bellowing-like sounds of his own snoring, grumbled during breakfast about the early morning avian cacophony. Justin was wearing his cycling gear as we all tucked into round after round of toast. Mal had convinced him that today's section was a much easier ride than the previous two, and so he agreed to join Mal in the day's mountain biking. The mood around the breakfast table was one of triumph at having crossed the Lake District without incident, and we had to slap ourselves mentally to remind us that we hadn't finished, we still had five days and over a hundred and something miles to go, and it wasn't going to be easy.

Justin looked apprehensive despite the rest of us reassuring him that he'd be all right. His bike was far too shiny having only been ridden once in New Zealand and once on the practice run, and it needed to be removed from the car roof and well and truly dirtied. After Andrea and I had visited Justin in New Zealand we couldn't understand how it was possible to own a mountain bike in that beautifully unspoilt wild country, arguably one of the best places in the world for riding such a machine, and only use it once. There should be a law against that kind of thing - criminal underuse of specialist recreational equipment in an area of outstanding natural suitability, punishable by forty lashes with a greasy bike chain. (I could think of more imaginative recrimination involving sprockets and orifices but these would likely result in the perpetrator's inability ever to ride a bike again. For the sake of decency I'll shuffle them back into the darker recess of my sub-consciousness.)

The weather was stuck in 'repeat' mode, it being hot and sunny again, so the chances of Justin's bike actually getting muddy were slim. After paying and thanking the landlord of the Mardale Inn for his fabulous food and accommodation the five of us loaded our gear into the car and were ready to go. Coated in Vaseline and sun cream, and with the Camelbaks loaded with drink, Vin and I were first to leave along the lane out of Bampton. The humpback bridge that yesterday was Everest had overnight flattened into Holland. Such is the nature of a bonk. I'd lent Vin my spare cap and we both sported headgear to keep off the fierce morning sun. Within half a mile the two cyclists, who were taking it easy and laughing over a shared joke, caught us. Andy's voice, sounding anxious, suddenly blasted from all our radios. "OK, who's gone off with the car keys?" It was Vin's and my turn to laugh as Justin grabbed his brakes and squeaked to a halt. Mal called Justin a "cabbage!" as he turned in the road and headed back to Bampton, pedalling faster than he had been a moment earlier. We ran on, chuckling to ourselves.

Justin was turning out to be the team 'all rounder', working as driver, navigator, chef and waiter, quartermaster, banker and now athlete, his general mild demeanor helping him slip effortlessly into any one of the roles. When the coast-to-coast was originally conceived he toyed with the idea of full time biker but considered the training required to be too time consuming so chose the multi-tasking option, and I have to say he filled the role magnificently.

Further up the lane heading towards the M6 motorway we cut off to the left on a footpath that took us up a grassy hill that was uneven and cut up underfoot by the hooves of cattle. The geology had changed noticeably. Not only were the hills smaller and significantly less steep but also small craggy white limestone outcrops were now evident in place of the darker rougher rocks previously encountered. Andy again called over the radio. It appeared we had all forgotten something. He put on his best DJ voice "Welcome to Radio Bondy here at Respect The Stupidity. It's another bright sunny morning. Here's some music for all you runners and riders out there". Through the speaker came the instantly recognisable sound of *Carmina Burana*. How could we have forgotten that before departure? The music stopped suddenly as Radio Andy shut down leaving us in peaceful silence bar a few bird sounds from the woodland up ahead.

After a short climb through grassy fields we started a steady descent beside a quarry that was enclosed by a thin strip of trees. My knee had just started to trouble me with the same pain from the descent to Bampton and I was about to grumble about it when our attention was caught by a stag sprinting through the narrow copse about 30 yards ahead. That took my mind off the pain, but not for long. A few minutes later we burst out of the woods into the sunlight and were hit by the roar of traffic hurtling up the motorway. After two days of mountain calm it was a rude awakening to be thrust back into 21st century car-riddled England. We stood for a minute or two on the bridge across the motorway, watching the traffic thunder dizzyingly along the tarmac, the smell of petrol and diesel fumes unpleasantly overpowering the rural freshness.

The following several miles involved running along predominantly straight tarmac lanes. It felt reminiscent of scenes from US road movies as the heat shimmered above the surface of the road stretching achingly into the distance. I was definitely feeling heavy legged, particularly in comparison to Vin who had recovered well from the previous two days, and I had to get him to slow the pace several times on even the slightest inclines. The conversation had dropped to the occasional few words, as we seemed to descend into a sort of running slumber, just ticking off the miles one by one. The navigation was unchallenging and there was little of visual note to grab our concentration. As a stimulus we challenged ourselves to run across the next road junction with our eyes closed. This may appear incredibly foolish. However, as we'd not seen any cars since the M6 half an hour ago, and the road was little more than single carriageway, we felt the most likely thing to trouble us would be the local vicar on his bike. We were wrong. It was more risky than we'd anticipated. Not because there was a threat of being hit by anything but because when we closed our eyes we both veered to the side and nearly ran straight into the dry stone wall on the other side of the lane, just realising what was about to happen at the last moment and swerving back onto the tarmac. As 'wild living' I don't pretend that it was in the same league as a cocaine-fuelled celebrity orgy or an insane high-speed joyride but hey, you get your kicks where you can, and at least it was legal.

The next car we saw was the crew car, approaching us from behind. Andy had the windows down enjoying the sunshine, and the stereo was on with good-time summer music blaring. He appeared very relaxed and content as he drove alongside us for two or three miles whilst we all chatted and listened to the radio. I had the small video camera in my pack, which I pulled out and did a little impromptu interview of Andy as we steadily ran along next to the car. He whizzed on a mile or so ahead and set up his large TV camera to film us approaching, and also to film Mal and Justin, who were still somewhere behind us as Mal had to stop when his sunglasses fell apart!

We were faced with a choice of route – stay on the lanes all the way to the lunch rendezvous or take a bridleway section through some thick woodland at Wyegill Plantation. We'd had enough of baking on the hot road for the time being and our ankles felt strong so the off-road route was chosen. The trail through the trees was overgrown, and wound its way past and over several fallen branches underneath a thick canopy that shut out much of the light. The air was cool, dank and musty, and the ground damp and soft, carpeted with pine needles. This was evidently favoured terrain of the deer, as we disturbed a further three of them, seeing two and hearing the third as it crashed away from us in a startled manner. By the time we exited the woods we both had several scratches down our legs from the undergrowth. This I was used to. My previous straight-line training across the heath land had paid off. After vaulting a gate the trail took us into open fields, and Vin suddenly called a halt, clenched his stomach, spun round and sprinted back into the woods. Here we go again, I thought. Not wishing to get inflammatory about his bowel syndrome I got myself comfortable in the grass, sat and waited, contentedly perusing the map. And the world was glorious! The sun shone a warming shine, birds sang, lambs gambled around their mothers who ate lush green grass, and everything was happy. I realised just how far away what we were doing was from the daily grind. And, although missing my family, I was thoroughly enjoying life on the run.

Vin reappeared. If we really had been 'on the run' it wouldn't have taken much of a bloodhound to follow our track. What with the scent trail Vin had been leaving since Rosthwaite we would more likely have been hunted down by the Andrex puppy.

The path we had to follow wound its way through numerous fields that all looked the same, some with sheep, some without. Some of the fences had stiles, the others not and it was all too easy to find ourselves stuck in a field with no obvious exit. It was midday before we ran down a farm lane and onto the road at Crosby Ravensworth where Andy was once again waiting to film us. We declined the offer of supplies, instead carrying on up the grassy climb to Bank Moor. Now I was feeling the strain. "That must be the top of the hill where the road is, there", Vin pointed, "where that blue Peugeot 306 is parked". Peugeot 306! Blue! I could barely make out the shape of something bulky on the skyline that I'd assumed was a rock, and here was 'Hawkeye' all but telling me its registration number. Up until now I'd thought my eyes were pretty good. Now I realised they weren't even pretty. As if to make me feel more inadequate he found it all too easy to run away from me up the hill, and I had neither the energy nor the will to try and stay with him. He waited for me at the top of the climb, sure enough standing next to a blue 306, before we hit the small lanes once more for the final two miles to the rendezvous. This was the worst I'd felt so far. The lanes were again straight and steadily uphill. If I looked into the distance my slow speed became evident and I had to keep my eyes on the ground a few feet in front of me to avoid getting demoralised. There were several skylarks hovering around us, their playful incessant chirruping sounding as if they were laughing and joking at my ordeal. The heat was at its most intense and I could feel it radiating onto my sore calves from the hot sticky tarmac. I tried to focus my mind; look down, one foot in front of the other, left, right, left right. Don't look ahead. Grey shoes slapping the road, left, right, left, right, slap, slap, slap, slap, shoe, road, shoe, road. The grass on the verge six inches to the side of my right foot looks brown and sun baked. Slap, slap, slap, slap…

I eventually looked up to see that I had dropped fifty yards or so behind Vin, and hoped that he would stop and wait for me as I'd finished off all the drink in my Camelbak. Thankfully it was only a few minutes before he slowed to allow me alongside, and did indeed offer me some fluid. On top of the hill we could see numerous craggy flat outcrops of rock all around that were 'limestone pavements' - flat sections of limestone exposed by the scouring action of glaciers. Once exposed the limestone is slowly eroded by corrosive draining of water along cracks, forming deep fissures called 'grykes' between standing flat slabs called 'clints'. If the grykes are straight and the clints uniform in size there is strong resemblance to man-made paving slabs, hence the geological feature has acquired the name limestone pavement.

Over the brow of the moor the road dropped downhill steeply but only for a short distance. There was a sudden worsening in my knee pain as I fought the gradient, and I could feel my gait altering to a limp until the road levelled again. I ignored the pain, my mind focused on refuelling at the rendezvous which we could now see a quarter of a mile ahead up a slight rise. Mal and Justin were sitting in the sun and Andy had his TV camera on his shoulder as we approached, Vin several yards in front and feeling fine, me lagging and limping behind. The two bikers were just about to leave but on seeing us approaching decided to stay by the car for a while longer and have a 'second sitting' of lunch.

Whilst we ate and refilled our Camelbaks Vin went straight into his elaborate stretching routine, entertaining us onlookers with his 'rubber-man' contortions, and providing an interesting photo opportunity. I felt too exhausted for any such activity, instead choosing to lie by the side of the road and take some painkillers with my food. We were situated on a narrow lane adjacent to a farm track that formed the next bridleway we were to take. Every few minutes a farmer sped in and out of the track in his larger-and-faster-than-usual tractor, almost sliding it round the corner, and throwing dust clouds into the air. He'd clearly done this thousands of times before and knew the racing line to take on the bend. However, the last thousands of times there hadn't been a very expensive mountain bike leaning against the dry stone wall just out of his line of vision, and Mal winced as the heavy thundering machine nearly ripped his steed to pieces and crushed it into the limestone. Fortunately it missed and the bike was quickly repositioned in a safer place.

We all took it slow and easy on this lunch break, making sure we'd eaten plenty and got some rest in. As we prepared to set off again we could see some ominous dark clouds forming in the direction we were heading, and the occasional flash of distant lightning. Cooler weather appeared to be on its way.

The runners and riders set off together up the farm track, and for the next couple of miles played leapfrog with each other at the innumerable gates that required opening and shutting. Vin and myself would reach a gate first, hold it open for Mal and Justin, who'd ride on to the next gate whilst we shut that one. Then they'd be opening the next and holding it for us to run through. This pattern remained unremarkable until we caught up with the bikers whilst they were standing by a gate and surveying the field ahead. Ten yards in front of them stood a huge bull. This was a gigantic car-sized black beast with a large ring through its nose and a noisy bellow that vibrated our chests and was getting louder and more frequent. The four of us stood together for a minute and debated the possible consequences of continuing through the field. The bull was slowly making its way towards us at the gate, every now and then turning from side to side to reveal its full size. Three of us were convinced it didn't want us to pass, and voted to jump over a fence into the next field that contained a flock of docile sheep (my first name may be Matt but my surname is not Ador!). Vin on the other hand, being more of a 'city boy', was all for running past the bull, proclaiming the line that may one day be his epitaph "We'll be all right, we'll outrun it!" I'd have liked to see this happen. Vin is fast at the best of times, and I was curious to find out just how fast he could be with the imminent prospect of a bovine horn vigorously rammed up his fast retreating rear end. Sensing his bravado the animal dropped his head and started pawing and scraping the ground with a front leg, as they do when faced by a matador. This suddenly brought about a unanimous verdict, and within a minute or so we'd all leapt the fence, passed the two bikes over and circumvented the problem animal with a quick stroll through the sheep's field. Once a safe distance past the bull we climbed back over a high dry stone wall to rejoin the trail. As we did so two mountain bikers came the other way towards us and we felt it right to warn them about the marauding meat mountain at the other end of the field. One of them agreed that climbing the wall was the best idea. The other, who was clearly of Vin's way of thinking, decided to stay on the path. We stood to watch from the higher ground that curved round the field like a natural amphitheatre, as if this was our coliseum and we the Emperors waiting to be entertained by the ensuing gladiatorial battle. Not so much Christians and lions as bikers and bull. The bull had lumbered twenty yards or so away from the gate by this point. The first biker slowed dramatically as he approached, keeping close to the edge of the field and giving the beast a wide berth. As the bull became aware of him it started bellowing again, and lumbered towards the gate. As quick as he could the biker dismounted, grabbed the gate and dragged his bike through before pulling it shut again. The Emperors cheered and gave a raised thumb; he battled, he triumphed, he is to live. The second biker had been watching and slowly following his colleague from a distance. Seeing his friend's success he too rode towards the gate, but the bull wasn't going to be caught out twice. From the high vantage point the Emperors were entertained as it walked right over to the gate and stood almost leaning against it, bellowing and staring at the approaching biker, who now stopped, rethinking his options. A death or glory onward lunge, or tail-between-the-legs tactical retreat! Slowly he dismounted and held his bike between himself and the snorting monster. The combatant had chosen his shield for the encounter. Expensive mountain bikes and five-bar gates are both designed to fulfill specific functions. One of the two is particularly good at keeping livestock where you want them. The other, sadly, isn't. The bull advanced. Within split seconds option one looked woefully lacking in the glory aspect and overburdened with the prospect of the death outcome, and was rapidly dismissed. In a flash the biker had turned, thrown his bike over the wall, climbed after it and rejoined his companion in the next field.

Score: bull 5, walkers and bikers 1.

The Emperors booed and hissed their disapproval at the displayed lack of courage and gratuitous bloodshed (having conveniently decided to forget their own lack of courage and gratuitous bloodshed not five minutes before) and gesticulated unanimous thumbs down.

The entertainment over, we continued on our way. The lunch break had been of great benefit to me, my legs improving dramatically. I was still a little hungry though, and took the advantage of an easy flat grassy section to chew on another sports energy bar.

The four of us exited the bridleway together, and the last five miles of the day involved a simple mostly-downhill stretch of road to the small town of Kirkby Stephen, which is situated in the Upper Eden valley surrounded by a landscape of pastoral rural scenery and wild uplands. Mal and Justin sped off leaving us two runners with a steady road run, which we completed in good time, particularly as the painkillers taken at the lunch stop had made my knee comfortable.

We had the grid reference of the bed and breakfast marked on our map, and as we turned the last corner we found the crew car parked up with the boot raised and our 'café' open. Andy, Mal and Justin were all sitting on the pavement with cups of tea and cake. We were quick to join them. Bizarrely, I thought I thought I saw four parrots flying overhead. I knew it had been hard work that day but surely not enough for a hallucinogenic bonk! At 22 miles distance and 3,000 feet of climbing this had been a relatively short day, but having immediately followed the Lakeland crossing it had still been a tough three hours and 33 minutes of running, gate opening and bull dodging.

We were staying in a large well-kept Georgian town house with four floors, high ceilings and ornate architraves and chandeliers. The owner's daughter had welcomed us in, showed us to our rooms and then served excellent tea and home-made cake in the impressive sitting room. We devoured them despite having spent half an hour or so 'grazing' from the back of the car. As usual Andy lost no time in connecting up the laptop and downloading the day's photos, before updating the website. After showering and cold soaking the legs we took the opportunity to wash some of our dirty gear, hanging it on the washing line in the large well-maintained garden to the rear of the property. Vin was taking it easy in the bath, enjoying a long hot soak. This isn't usually the best way to recover from a long run as the warmth can exacerbate any inflamed tissues, and I was concerned that he was making a big mistake.

Although it had become overcast, the weather was still warm and the threatening thunderstorms had moved away. As the late afternoon progressed, the clouds dispersed producing another warm evening with deep blue clear skies, suggesting another sunny day to follow. Justin, Mal and myself sat in the evening sunshine on some stone steps next to the garden, and checked the maps for the following day's routes. Mal had also been for a short walk around the town, a traditional market town of historic buildings, cobbled yards, quaint corners and interesting shops. He had found a cheap and cheerful fish and chip café. This was chosen as the place to eat our evening meal – plenty of carbohydrate, minimum cost, minimum fuss, and also turned out to be Vin's first experience of mushy peas. Although being Dutch he had lived most of his life in England

and had managed to reach the age of 28 before indulging in the delicacy. One mouthful and he proclaimed never to eat them again, preferring his baked bean option. Walking back from the fish and chip shop I again noticed the parrots that were now screeching and flying above the rooftops of the main street, and pointed them out to my colleagues just to confirm my sanity. Everyone agreed they were indeed parrots, and Mal had seen them previously on his trip into town. We were now all concerned. The first night we were woken by sheep, the next night by birds, and there was a definite possibility that tonight's sleep could be disturbed by parrots! It was getting more bizarre. What could tomorrow bring?

oooOooo

Mal, Vin and Matt share a joke on the beach at St Bees

Checking the map at Honister slate mine

Watendlath Tarn. Borrowdale in the background

Weary! Pit-stop at Patterdale

Feeding frenzy at Bampton

Surrender Bridge

Day 4. Friday 12th May 2006. Kirkby Stephen to Reeth.
23 miles

Fortunately the night was a calm and peaceful one animal-wise, but I still didn't sleep well. I had been restless, yet tried to lie as still as possible, firstly to aid relaxation and secondly to prevent noises from the old creaky bed I occupied waking Justin, with whom I again shared a room. A couple of times in the night I had to get up to use the toilet (I'd obviously re-hydrated well) and was worried that the groaning of the bare, slightly uneven floorboards and squeaking bedroom door hinges would rouse all the incumbents of the distinguishly aged property. I needn't have worried. During conversation over the immaculate antique hardwood table in the ground floor dining room at breakfast nobody claimed to have heard either me, or the parrots. The owner of the property had returned late at night from London where she'd been watching a cricket match, and now served us the best scrambled eggs on toast we'd ever experienced.

Today's stage had been highlighted as the 'swampy' one. We had tried to research the intricacies of the route across the country, paying attention to gradients, altitudes, distances and terrain. According to our colleagues in the walking fraternity, from whom we'd sought opinions via an Internet chat forum, the only significantly boggy section would be on Nine Standards Rigg, between Kirkby Stephen and Keld. From the dining room window we could see up the large climb towards Nine Standards, and whilst it appeared benign under the clear skies of yet another warm and sunny early summer morning, we had been warned. A change in footwear was decided. The previous three days of firm rocky terrain and hard grassland had been well suited to my 'New Balance' trail shoes that were extremely snug fitting around my unusually narrow feet, but had a less aggressive tread pattern than my 'Saucony' trail shoes. The latter were chosen to carry me over Nine Standards Rigg, as they would offer greater grip on muddy surfaces. The trade-off was that they were a little wider in the forefoot and had in the past been a factor in causing blisters. I was fairly confident that my feet were now tough enough not to succumb to blisters, but to be sure I took extra care when lathering on the Vaseline.

Both pairs of trail shoes were fairly new, being bought within the previous three months, yet were well 'worn-in' as a result of my high training mileage. The previous pair (also made by New Balance) had served me excellently, had covered more than the expected average lifetime distance of 500 miles, and were well travelled having been on the trip to New Zealand. I'd worn them for a workout in the hotel gym during our stopover in Bali, and for a similar workout in Singapore on the return journey. Before they left England I had given them a thorough clean, and had packed them in the top of my suitcase for good reason. I had been warned that New Zealand immigration were extremely keen on bio-security issues, and would want to inspect any equipment previously used in rural or remote countryside. This was indeed the case, and prior to being accepted into the country I had to produce my trail shoes for inspection by the immigration official. I'm sure her job had many moments of excitement and pleasantness. This wasn't one of them. I apologised for the malodorous state of my excessively sweated-in footwear, this despite them being visually clean, and continued to answer several questions regarding the terrain in which I had used the shoes. Happy that I wasn't a bio-terrorist or likely to wreak ecological havoc throughout vast swathes of antipodean countryside (despite wreaking havoc with the olfactory ambience in Wellington airport arrivals area) the official wished us a happy holiday and waved us through, no doubt before immediately rushing off to wash her hands and apply copious quantities of sweetly smelling nosegay.

I was able to get in a handful of runs during our stay, although not as many as I would have liked and no really long runs through the fantastic mountainous countryside. But this was a family holiday after all and not a running trip. We were holidaying in Nelson at the northern tip of South Island, staying with Justin and his partner Clare, who were working in New Zealand for a year. They were renting a small yet lovely house that was situated three hundred vertical feet up a steep, narrow winding driveway, hanging on a mountainside, with a fabulous ocean view. Perfect for hill sprint training. I could jog steadily down to the ocean then sprint back up. This climb took around four and a half minutes. Half a dozen repeats of this and I was ready to throw up. But the most enjoyable runs were the ones along the oceanfront. One particular eight-miler was back to their house from the hospital in Nelson where Clare worked. The run started just before sundown, and I was running along the side of the ocean as the flaming orange sun slowly plunged behind it, scorching the sky into ribbons of red and pink interspersed with deep blue, and producing one of the most startling sunsets I have ever seen. The combination of the view, the fresh sea air, the exercise and having a fantastic time on the other side of the world made this one of the best running experiences of my life.

The post-holiday blues were blown away with the running of the Chatsworth Challenge race in early September – the 26 miles for which I'd checked the route the day before my cardiac ultrasound scan. Vin came over to Chesterfield to stay with us the night before, as he was doing the run as well. We started well, reaching the top of the first significant hill from Baslow to Eagle Stone together and out in the lead. Deciding to slow a little to pace ourselves better we were caught up by another two runners as we traversed Curbar Edge, and stayed as a group of four for the next fifteen miles or so, pleasantly chatting among ourselves (this was a very informal 'race', more of a group run). Vin and the other two guys stayed pretty much together, whereas I'd drop back on the climbs but then have no difficulty in passing them on the descents, invariably reaching the bottom of each hill first. After sixteen miles I was starting to flag, and sent Vin on ahead with the other two runners, with the instruction to win the race. Six miles from the finish I was passed by another runner who had paced himself well and was catching the three leaders. I eventually dragged myself to the finish in fifth place, several minutes ahead of the sixth place runner, and in a time ten minutes faster than that of my practice run. Vin finished in joint first place after a sprint to the line. He'd done well, but I had ammunition to tease him from the fact that his co-winner was apparently still suffering from a hangover from two nights before, AND had cycled thirty miles from Derby that morning to get to the start. The Chatsworth Challenge is an excellently run event, suitable for walkers as well as runners, follows a beautiful course and has free tea, cakes and soft drinks at each checkpoint – worth entering for that alone.

By October I was looking to replace the trusty yet worn trail shoes, and had bought some fell racing shoes from a shop in Keswick during a trip to the Lake District with Mal and our respective ladies. I'd been swayed by their ultra-aggressive no-slip tread and slipper-like foot hugging comfort. The grip was phenomenal, and it was the purchase of this footwear that led to my next significant injury. Keen to test out the traction over steep terrain I ran from home to some local reservoirs in Linacre Woods for a hill session – sprinting straight up the very steep grassy side of the dam wall. The shoes gripped phenomenally well and I managed half a dozen repeats of the 30-second 'eyeballs out, lung busting' uphill sprint, with every step trying to rip my Achilles tendon apart from the excessive forces thrusting with my foot flexed at the steep angle required to power me up the bank. This was foolish. By the end of the last repetition not only was I feeling very dizzy and nauseous from the effort (this I expected) but also I had a pain at the back of my left ankle stretching into my lower calf. I jogged home very cautiously but the pain remained. After some thought I suspected Achilles tendonitis and prescribed myself a week of rest, iced my ankle four times a day and took anti-inflammatories. A week later I attempted a 'trial' run, but foolishly wore the fell shoes again as I had fallen in love with their comfort and grip. As soon as I set off the pain returned, but more foolishly I tried to run through it gently. This was unsuccessful, and I put myself through another two weeks of rest, ice and anti-inflammatories before finally doing something sensible and arranging to see a sports podiatrist.

The podiatrist was also a keen runner. He listened to my story, prodded, poked, looked hard and got me to stand in various positions. I'd had the forethought to take all my running shoes with me for him to examine. One look at my new fell shoes with his expert eye and he was able to show me the problem. The height of the heel was a good half an inch lower than on my trail shoes. This decreased the angle between my foot and shin when I ran uphill, putting extra strain on the Achilles tendon. When I sprinted up the very steep gradient of the dam wall the forces in my Achilles were more than it could take and he confirmed that I had indeed injured my Achilles tendon, probably causing a partial rupture. This was not good news. The Achilles tendon is extremely slow to heal, if it heals at all. There was a strong possibility that my foolishness had ruled me out of starting the coast-to-coast after nearly a year of preparation. I was advised of several things; firstly to get an ultrasound scan of the tendon to assess the degree of damage; secondly, to get advice from a sports physiotherapist regarding a rehabilitation program; thirdly, to wear heel-raise inserts in all my shoes to reduce the stretch on the damaged tendon.

The first two tasks were quite easy for me being in the fortunate position of working in the ultrasound department of a district general hospital and having several friends in the physiotherapy department. I was annoyed at not having already thought of doing this. I initially performed the ultrasound scan myself, and sure enough there was a black 'blob' on the screen midway down the tendon. This corresponded to an area of fluid and close scrutiny of the fibres in that area confirmed a partial tear. I sought an opinion from one of the Consultant Radiologists who specialises in musculo-skeletal ultrasound; he confirmed my initial diagnosis.

The next task was to telephone a friend of mine, Alan Ward, who is not only a senior physiotherapist but also the captain of Dark Peak fell running club. He did not specialise in sports injuries himself but gave me the number of his colleague, Mick Heys, who agreed to see me later that week.

Things started to look up with Mick's consultation. I was very reassured to hear him say that there was no reason why I wouldn't be able to run 180 miles in six months time, provided I followed the program of exercises he prescribed. These were not to repair the torn fibres – that would possibly never happen. Instead the plan was to make the intact fibres stronger such that they would be more than able to compensate for the torn ones. I'd been given a chance to be fit to run and I wasn't going to blow it. Every opportunity I had, whether at work or at home, I was to be found performing the exercises, bobbing up and down, pushing walls or generally stretching my calves. An early Christmas present from my parents was a pack of BioFlow magnets, two of which I positioned in my sock either side of the tendon to try and speed up the healing and strengthening process.

By mid December I was feeling more strength and less discomfort in the Achilles region. During the rehabilitation period I'd tried to maintain my level of cardio-vascular fitness by swimming. I'd get into the pool and swim non-stop for 90 minutes or so, only getting out when my throat was sore from the chlorine. Whether this was beneficial with regards to the coast-to-coast is debatable, but at least my swimming style improved dramatically. I felt ready to run again but had to stop risking injury and sort out a coherent training plan.

oooOooo

Mal was first away out of Kirkby Stephen, on his own as Justin had rejoined Andy on the support crew. We runners set off a few minutes later, jogging down the main street before turning right over the River Eden and starting the long climb up Nine Standards. This was steep at first, up a road that wound clockwise around a deep working quarry. We adopted a jog / walk pattern, conserving energy on the steeper sections and picking up time on the lesser gradient. The road ended and gave way to a wide well-defined bridleway, the surface of which was predominantly firm and rocky. We could see the summit a long way ahead, nine protrusions penetrating the skyline at a height of 2172 feet (662m) above sea level. The trail ran alongside a stream that was almost completely dry following the good weather. This was a good sign – maybe it wouldn't be as boggy as we'd been warned. The sun was still shining on us but there was a stiffer breeze, thankfully now blowing from the west, assisting our ascent. As we turned off the main track onto a narrow path heading for the summit we realised our good fortune. It was dry, the firm peat having just a little spring underfoot, like running on a carpet with extra layers of underlay below. Every twenty metres or so stepping-stones and boardwalks were held tight in the set earth, reminders that most of the time this was wet swampy bog. The incline had levelled off a little and we were making far better time than our wildest expectations. We reached the summit within 45 minutes of setting off, and stood admiring the nine man-made stone columns that were built in a line a few yards apart along the mountaintop and all towered above our heads. The origin of the nine "stone men" is a mystery, and some of the columns, which are about ten feet tall, were in a perilous state until repair work was carried out in 2005. According to Wainwright they are ancient and are marked on 18th century maps. One theory is that the Roman army built them to look like troops from a distance. The trig point at the summit of Nine Standards Rigg marks the watershed divide across England, from this point rivers flow west toward the Irish Sea and east toward the North Sea.

The wind strengthened and for the first time since leaving St Bees we were a little cold, choosing to stand behind one of the stacks and send a couple of text messages to Mal and the crew.

We had a route option from the summit – a fairly easy way down followed by a longer road section, or a moorland descent to Whitsundale Beck then following the stream towards the River Swale and Keld. Buoyed by the firmer than expected terrain we chose the latter, and spent a few minutes using the compass, making sure we had found the correct tiny path down from the featureless (apart from the nine standards and the trig point) plateau.

There were a few wet gullies that we still had to cross, some of which would have sunk us well beyond our knees in sticky slimy stinking peat bog had we not carefully chosen our footings, and this gave us some idea of what it would be like following a wet spell. But on the whole the descent was easy and fast. Easy that is until my knee started to trouble again. It became known as my 'knee pixie' as I'd described it to Vin as having a pixie hanging onto my leg that hammered a nail under my kneecap every time I took a step. It was getting steadily worse throughout the downhill to Whitsundale Beck. As we reached and followed the stream southeasterly towards Keld the pain became extremely unpleasant. There were still several miles to go before the rendezvous where I could take some painkillers, and for the first time since Tuesday I had stopped enjoying running. It had become an ordeal but there was no option but to grit my teeth and carry on. What started out as a minor niggle two days ago was now a major concern. This wasn't supposed to happen. All along I was half prepared for a flare up of my ankle or Achilles injuries to cause trouble, but something new was harder to cope with. It was an unknown quantity. To add to the discomfort this section of trail was a far harder run than it appeared on the map. Rather than following a straight line alongside Whitsundale Beck as we had expected, every hundred yards or so the trail turned back up the gradient to cross much smaller streams that had cut deep into the hillside. This significantly added to the distance we had to run, and slowed us down as each stream crossing offered a variety of challenges, narrow twists, off-camber sections, steep dips and climbs, bogs and slippery stones, and each change in direction or gradient exacerbated the knee pain. As the beck's floodplain widened and the trail levelled I called a time-out and the two of us stopped by a stile. The wind was getting stronger and a few small clouds chased each other like children across a playground sky. I rubbed my knee and cursed while Vin engaged in another bout of elaborate stretching. The last half hour had been far harder than anticipated. And it had all been downhill.

For the first time doubts about our invincibility began to creep perniciously into my mind, tiny fissures of uncertainty in the mental armour I had layered around the belief that our running across the country was not only a possibility, but a foregone conclusion. I rubbed the offending joint again. It still hurt. We weren't even half way to Robin Hood's Bay. I looked over at Vin who still had the relaxed, almost blasé expression of someone deeply entrenched in their comfort zone, calm and undisturbed. Many people had used the word madness when we described our plans to run coast-to-coast. It now struck me that perhaps we were engaged in madness after all. Maybe they were right. Who were we to think we could run seven off-road marathons in seven consecutive days. I stretched my thigh muscles, and then rubbed my knee again. It looked normal but didn't hurt any less. Vin bobbed comically up and down, wearing the look of ignorant bliss of a fatted cow ambling its way happily to the abattoir. Of course it was madness, but the current pains could just be a minor setback. I endeavoured to cast the doubts to the wind and focused on the belief that we'd succeed. Trying to ignore the internal grindings of my left lower leg we set off again. Whitsundale met Swale and we turned east into Swale Dale, the river valley that would be our companion for the next day and a half. The River Swale was in its first flush of youth here, having been born from the marriage of Birkdale Beck and Great Sleddale Beck just one mile to the west.

Once on the short road section near Keld the level smooth surface caused a welcome dramatic decrease in pain. Radio contact was made with the crew who were waiting for us on a bridge over the river. They had only just arrived there having tended to Mal who had already passed through his arranged meeting point at the Tan Hill Inn a few miles to the north. His route for the day differed from ours as we had been predominantly using tiny footpaths on which bikes are not permitted. His alternative route took him on an arc of bridleways to the north east out of Kirkby Stephen through a Scrabble-game of amusing place names including Woofer Gill and High Greygrits to Tan Hill, then south easterly via Mirk Fell Edge, Great Scollit Hill, Tongue End and Moulds Bottom to Reeth. At least that was his plan.

Our rendezvous point had been chosen specifically to be by the river so that we could jump in and clean ourselves of the mud from the boggy moorland before changing clothes for the next leg. Andy and Justin were ready to film two swamp monsters as we reached them, but thanks to the dry conditions a dip in the river was disappointingly not necessary. We approached them along a narrow path on the North side of the Swale. Suddenly I experienced a swift sharp worsening of the pain in my knee, severe enough to stop me in my tracks with a yelp. Concerned but continuing we both made it to the crew car and I collapsed beside it, demanding some painkillers from the first aid box.

The journey into Swale Dale had not been without a significant amount of discomfort, but the beauty of the valley was a wonderful calming influence; the constant babbling of the fast flowing river in harmony with the wide variety of birdsong and bleating lambs. Lapwings called overhead, and were partially drowned out as the boiling kettle whistled. We were about a mile to the west of Keld, the village that represents the halfway point on the coast-to-coast crossing. Whilst we rested and ate, served as usual by the ever-reliable Justin, Andy was observed meddling around the front of his car. Every now and again the recognisable sound of gaffa tape being torn from the roll broke the peaceful lunchtime calm. The occasional giggle gave us the clue that he was up to something. Justin ventured round the front of the vehicle and found him taping wires to the bodywork. In the radiator grill was lodged his small 'marker pen' sized video camera and the wires led to equipment in the glove box. This could only mean one thing – some filming whilst driving. This filled the usually reserved Justin with dread. Andy drove fast at the best of times. A camera in the front of the car meant a sure-fire increase in speed and, on the narrow winding roads of the Yorkshire Dales, a likely pant-filling experience for Justin in the passenger seat. We wished him good luck and set off towards the steep climbs and descents of Gunnerside Moor, unaware that it was all about to go horribly wrong.

oooOooo

We sensed a significant moment as we passed the village of Keld and crossed a well-used trail that was heading north to south and that bore a marker post proclaiming "Pennine Way". It somehow represented a tangible mid-way point, and we were now nearer the East coast than the West, halfway through Day 4, on target for our seven-day finish. Ahead and down to the right flowed the Swale, already a hundred or so feet below, and half to the left and rising above us stood the high moors. Twisting northwards into the valley of Swinner Gill the path became very narrow, hanging on the steep hillside, a dizzying drop down into the narrow stream-cut valley to our right. The easterly climb out of the valley was long and very steep, pulling our pace back to a brisk walk with myself in front. Vin had started to go quiet again and I assumed it was just ebb in the conversation, a result of us having spent so much time together over the past few days. A couple of times I tried to kick-start the chat, asking him about his plans to buy a new motorbike, then about favourite music, even our liking for the TV sit-com *Game On*. It has been said that I bear a startling resemblance to one of the characters in *Game On*. Hopefully the likeness relates to the facial features of the actor who plays him, called Neil Stuke, rather than the character who is a disastrously mixed up over confident somewhat perverted agoraphobic, pathetically describing himself as a "double-hard bastard", with a hopeless obsession for the character played by Samantha Janus. So nothing like me then!

Out there on the moors there's no way I could have been accused of being agoraphobic!

Vin's replies to all my questions were short, with no elaboration to the basic response. Near the top of the climb I suspected he was having some kind of trouble that he hadn't told me about, so I asked if he was OK. He wasn't. His left thigh muscle was giving him a lot of pain, going into spasm just above the knee. This had come on quickly at the bottom of the climb and gave him trouble walking. I looked at his face and outwardly he still gave the appearance of comfort and confidence, but his eyes gave the game away, somehow looking darker. The ho-hum nonchalance had been usurped by oh-my-god soreness. On reaching the brow of the hill the footpath joined a wide gravel track that stretched for as far as we could see along the almost-flat moor. This was clearly a road used to transport well-to-do 'sportsmen' onto the moor to the shooting hides during the grouse season, and should have provided us with fast easy running. We attempted to increase the pace to a run, but Vin immediately began to limp and asked for a stop to rest and stretch his thigh muscles. There was a good breeze still blowing from behind us, which was welcome, as we'd sweated on the climb, and there was again no shade from the sun.

Off to our right the heat haze shimmered above the green-brown heather, giving the appearance of waves on the distant Moss Dam. We set off once more, although within a few strides Vin's limp was again evident, and as the track started to descend very slightly my knee pixie begin hammering a larger, and this time red-hot, nail under my kneecap. Now we were both limping, left leg bad, right leg good, on top of a baking desolate Yorkshire moor, with well over ten miles still to go to Reeth. Within half a mile we stopped again for Vin to stretch. As soon as we stopped my pain halted, but every time we set off it was excruciating for the first twenty steps or so, then eased to just about bearable. Another quarter of a mile, another stop to stretch! I was in less discomfort while we continued running but this was impossible for my companion. The stop, stretch, start, agony cycle continued until the next big challenge, which was the crossing of another steep and deep stream valley called Gunnerside Beck. There was no way round. The route options looked limited on the map, but as we crested the valley edge we could see several well-worn trails winding down both sides of the gorge to what appeared to be disused ramshackle quarry buildings. As soon as the trail steepened we were both in agony, wincing in pain as we half-limped and half-hopped down towards the stream bed. Vin appeared to be having more trouble than myself as once again he had dropped back, and kept stopping. I was in no position to say it, being in trouble myself, but I wondered whether this was the result of his hot soak in the bath the night before. I reached the old stone bridge that spanned the rushing stream, wedged claustrophobically in the valley bottom, and sat there, studying the map, waiting for Vin as he battled agonisingly with the force of gravity to finish his pained descent. Within the space of an hour's running we had gone from jovial indomitability to downcast impending failure. It was clear that our respective leg problems were not going to abate that day and for both of us finishing the coast to coast was suddenly in serious jeopardy. If this were a boxing match the referee would be preparing to step in and stop the bout. We were on the ropes and taking punches. This, however, was no place to throw in the towel. Like it or not we had to get to Reeth. For us both the pain was most severe on downhill sections. The vast majority of the route to Reeth was downhill; the last ten miles were simply a case of grin-and-bear-it damage limitation. A dark sense of humour took over with the next conversation:

Me: "Do you want the good news or the bad news?"

Vin: "What's the bad news?"

Me: "I've just been looking at the map. After we've got over this next hill we've got to struggle through at least six miles of downhill."

Vin: " What's the good news?"

Me: "Just over this hill we've got a fantastic six mile downhill!"

Pause.

Both of us: "BRILLIAAAANT!!!"

At the time we both laughed but afterwards Vin confessed to having wanted to punch my lights out.

The trail up the other side of the valley zigzagged through loose rock and scree before turning straight up the fall line on a less steep grassier surface. Over the top the long steady gradual downhill stretched in front of us as far as we could see. The whole of the hillside had been ravaged by centuries of lead mining activity and was all grey, uneven and covered in shale, with little vegetation. The lead ore galena had been mined in Swaledale for thousands of years. Such was the historical importance of the area that even the Romans knew of it and used it. Many derelict and ramshackle stone buildings remain littered across the scarred landscape, some of which represent a tombstone-like gate-house to shafts still dangerously penetrating the raped hillside, and all bearing testament to the unimaginably hard lives of the men who for generations lived, worked and died in the mines. The last man to mine Gunnerside Moor, John Thomas Rutter, died in 1975 aged 90. Passing some of the bleak, exposed, element-scoured ruins of what were accommodation units it was hard to imagine a more grim and dangerous existence. Somehow it seemed appropriate for us to be suffering painfully as we battled through Gunnerside; limping at a slow jog through the moonscape, feeling like injured time-travellers running to escape some strange alien beast. Ordinarily we would have been comfortably running each mile in less than eight minutes on this stretch, but were reduced to a pedestrian eleven minutes, more due to Vin's thigh than my knee. Every time the track steepened, even slightly, he had to slow down and this caused me more pain than running at my own pace. After a mile or so we reviewed the map. We were making very poor progress and decided to split up and run at our own pace and meet where the track opened out onto a small road at the appropriately named Surrender Bridge. I ran on ahead, leaving Vin to his hobble, and after twenty minutes or so I crashed out by the road and lay in the sun, eating a banana and taking on fluid whilst I waited for the arrival of the (usually) flying Dutchman. Some time later he joined me and I cruelly captured his grimacing limping arrival on video.

Just before we set off along the roads to Reeth, which was still three miles away at the junction between Swaledale and Arkengarthdale, I sent a text message to the rest of the team saying that we were in trouble at Surrender Bridge, but were carrying on regardless. As we ran I had time to do a bit more videoing, filming a brace of lapwings as they squawked and danced erratically overhead in an aerial dogfight. Now out of Gunnerside the hills were completely vegetated and far more pleasing to the eye, although the breeze and isolation still produced an atmosphere of bleakness. I could imagine that in winter the wind and snow would scythe harshly through all but the sturdiest of shelter. My comfortable pace was faster than that of Vin and I would run ahead and film whilst he passed me, then catch him and run ahead again. As I stood watching him approach the crew car came into view behind him. Concerned at our text message Andy and Mal, who had just finished his days biking, had jumped into the car and set off in our direction. It took them a few minutes to find Surrender Bridge on the map, as I'd not sent a grid reference. On reaching the bridge and finding us gone they'd taken the shortest route towards Reeth and had no trouble catching us struggling downhill. With only a relatively short distance to go both Vin and I refused the offer of a lift (I'd vowed not to get into the crew car until Robin Hood's Bay). An agreement was made. I'd run on ahead to finish the stage at my least painful pace whilst Mal walked with Vin to give him support. Once we re-started, Andy whizzed past in the car to be ready for our arrival at the bed and breakfast.

The next half an hour or so into Reeth was very uncomfortable. I tried desperately to keep running at a slow steady pace to minimise the knee pain, but was forced into several periods of walking which initially felt more comfortable but not for long. Each time I returned to a jog the stinging worsened. The route was far from pleasant. Isolation became rat-run at the bottom of the sleepy lane, with a left hand turn at Healaugh onto the B6270, a major local road that had no footpath. Sharing the all-too-narrow carriageway with speeding cars and thundering lorries was a disconcerting experience that added a not insignificant degree of mental discomfort to the physical pain. Despite running in the cracked uneven gutter and brushing against walls and thorny hedgerows I often had to hold a hand out to the side to enable oncoming vehicles to see me sooner, allowing them more time to swerve and thus avoid turning me into roadkill, fine examples of which I regularly had to jump over or splat through. On rare occasions when I could admire the view instead of concentrate on the traffic I could see the Swale to my right still escorting us but now looking more serene and mature than it did at Keld. The water was smoother and calm, embraced by a wider flood plain of lush grass and farmland. It looked perfect for a lazy Sunday afternoon picnic, but I didn't have the opportunity to think of lying on a blanket next to a hamper bursting with victuals whilst the children giggled and played. There were many route opportunities along the riverbank but this would have risked lengthening the distance and increasing the pain on uneven ground. It was now a matter of survival, and with this thundering traffic, survival in the physical sense as well as metaphorical. On the outskirts of Reeth I was caught up in a melee of children and parents buzzing around a knot of randomly parked cars that slowed the flow of traffic and threatened to clot one of the major arteries into the village. I didn't have to look at my watch to know that it was around three-thirty in the afternoon and the school run was in full swing. After weaving between the mini-human ping-pong balls clothed in matching checked dresses or black trousers and running random rings around clucking mothers I crossed the road to the safety of a footpath that lasted all the way to our destination. Another steep downhill, a right bend and I was on the large village green, surrounded by 18th century houses. The town initially served the needs of the local farming community, but also became a centre for the local lead industries and also hand-knitting. Reeth has also played host to many films and TV series, most notably *All Creatures Great and Small.*

Our accommodation was situated on the far side of Reeth and the last two hundred yards were down a very steep road that caused me so much pain I had tears in my eyes as I hopped hopelessly along. On finally reaching the destination I sat in the road by the crew car utterly relieved as taking the weight off my leg made me instantly pain free. The car was safely parked at the end of a gravel lane across the road from our lodgings, next to it stood a stone built outhouse in which were safely stored the two mountain bikes. Justin was inside the bed and breakfast so I was served by Andy, who kept delving into the cool box, as all I wanted was yogurt and rice pudding. It was becoming increasingly difficult to imagine we'd be able to run well the next day, and as Vin hauled himself agonisingly into view fifteen minutes later and headed straight into the B+B after very little conversation it was looking very much like the end of our adventure. Before switching off the GPS watch for a recharge I noted that it had taken us the very slow time of five hours and nine minutes to run / walk / limp the 23 miles containing 4000 feet of climbing and painful descending.

Either through denial or a sense of team spirit, morale remained high, and we still congratulated each other on a job well done. Mal had ridden well through a difficult navigation stage where the bridleways he intended to take kept petering out on top of featureless heather moorland. He described them as 'Ninja Trails', one minute they were there, the next they were gone. Yet he had still found his way down into Reeth, albeit via a modified, confused and made-up-on-the-spot route. He was confidently ticking each stage off with no significant mishaps. His biggest problem was keeping his map case in one piece and fastened to his bike, it now being held together with a large amount of gaffa tape. (Mal had previously challenged Andy to find a source of gaffa tape in remote North Yorkshire, and shouldn't really have been surprised to find he already had a stock in the boot of the car.)

Coming to Vin's rescue had, however, been slightly traumatic for Mal. He had climbed into the crew car passenger seat and was sitting holding a cup of tea whilst casually searching the map for the location of Surrender Bridge. Andy, sensing a heightened state of urgency, leapt into the driving seat, fired up the engine and accelerated the car at high speed up the hill out of Reeth. The sudden unexpected motion resulted in the boiling hot contents of Mal's cup being sprayed into the air and down into his groin, a highly sensitive area that was protected only by a thin layer of entirely non-heat-resistant lycra. He danced and squirmed with scalded genitalia whilst wrestling with an opened map as Andy continued his high-speed rescue drive, a drive that was heading in any random direction as Surrender Bridge had still not been located. Mal had also removed his dirty cycling socks at the bed and breakfast before quickly throwing back on just his rigid-soled biking shoes for the rescue attempt. This made for an uncomfortable walk back to Reeth with Vin, and on inspecting his feet later Mal found two blisters. He made a mental note always to wear the correct footwear in future, and, more importantly, never to hold a cup of hot liquid over his gonads whilst sitting in a vehicle.

The crew had been faultless in their support once again, and had both survived the unofficial 'rallying' to get the best effect from the car-mounted camera. This video was now being played on the television in the triple room that we three athletes were sharing, the mini-video camera connected to the TV above my bed. I was lying feet elevated and with an ice pack around my left knee. Credit again to the crew for acquiring a bag full of ice for me at a moment's notice. Despite the pain I'd experienced whilst running I was glad that I had been on foot and not in the car. It looked quite a ride. When the ice pack had melted I showered and sprayed cold water on my legs for as long as I could stand it. Then for good measure I wrapped a towel round my upper body, took a cup of hot tea with me and sat in an empty bath. I switched on just the cold tap and let it run until the chilled water slowly rose to the level of my waist, entirely covering my legs that by this time appeared somewhat blue and mottled. There I sat for twenty minutes, determined to get as much benefit from the short recovery period as possible. I'm not sure I'd recommend this as a leisure activity, except perhaps for the pathologically bizarre. When I stoop up to get out of the bath my body below the waist was completely white, looking like it belonged to some kind of tailor's albino mannequin. An androgynous one! It would have taken an experienced genito-urologist with perfect eyesight and a magnifying glass to have confidently determined my gender.

For the evening meal and briefing for day five we all strolled back up the hill to a pub on the village green. We were fortunate to acquire a large enough table for all five of us to sit round and lay out maps to check optimistically the following days route. As usual we ate until we could eat no more, replenishing our bodies' glycogen stores so that we had the energy levels to haul them along for another day, even though their bio-mechanics were threatening catastrophic failure. On leaving the pub there was clearly a significant change in the weather. The temperature had dropped dramatically and a thick mist had descended, reducing the visibility to a couple of hundred yards. It was a minor shock to the system after the mini-heatwave previously experienced and there was a collective shiver, as we all felt underdressed on the short walk back. A short walk that was just about as painful for me as the finish of the day's run. Despite the rest period and cold soaking, my left knee was still unable to take my weight on a descent without severe pain, even at walking speed. I knew what I needed to do and that was to contact Mad Dog for his expert advice. He'd sort me out, but that required access to the internet, something which was currently proving impossible. There were no mobile or landline telephone signals in Reeth as apparently a transmitter had been knocked out by a thunderstorm. I limped back down to the bed and breakfast as uncomfortably, yet much slower, than I had a few hours earlier. With the longest distance to run tomorrow the situation wasn't looking good.

oooOooo

Mad Dog and Englishmen

Day 5. Saturday 13th May 2006. Reeth to Ingleby Cross
33 miles

I woke to the sound of my alarm clock beeping at six-thirty in the morning following the first restful night's sleep of the trip. Instead of the usual early morning cheerful chorus of birdsong the dominant sound was a much darker one of rain hammering on the window. A poke of the head through the curtains adjacent to my bed confirmed the weather to be dull, grey, misty and rainy. I couldn't see as far as our new friend the Swale although I knew she was out there in the fog, meandering timelessly onward untroubled by the elements. My first thoughts were in deciding what to wear to run in, as I couldn't guess the outside air temperature. Shorts or leggings, T-shirt or long sleeves? This train of thought was soon derailed as I put feet to the floor and felt the sharp stabbing pain around my stiffened knee, which screamed through my skull "Remember me?". It wasn't as intense as at the end of the previous day's run but there appeared to be significantly less mobility in the joint. Would I be running at all? More importantly could I get downstairs for breakfast? Several minutes were spent on the floor with my usual stretching routine and a few extra moves were included to try and loosen the painful joint. This was far from easy. Mal, Vin and I were sharing a room that was just large enough for three single beds and the squeezed-in en-suite. Floor space was at a premium, and what space there was tended to consist of narrow alleyways with right-angled bends. Each change of stretch required a change of position within the room, as if I were the final piece of a giant jigsaw trying to prove it could force its way into any available space to complete the puzzle. On the floor was the best place to be, however. With three men in the room all night, all of whom had been indulging in a program of excessive exercising and eating, the ambience was a little 'ripe'. The cooler air near the carpet was far more pleasing to the nose than the warm toxic fog closer to the ceiling. It's a good job none of us smoke. Any spark would have blown the windows out. Mal and Vin were also now stirring, stretching and generally preparing to go to breakfast. Vin worked hard stretching his left thigh muscle. As we walked down the stairs to the breakfast room I had great trouble taking the weight on my left knee whenever my right foot went down to the next step. Today was scheduled to be the longest in terms of distance, an ultra-marathon at 33 miles. I had never run this far before.

Ultra-marathons are generally considered to be any distance longer than the standard marathon distance of 26 miles and 385 yards. The shortest ultra-marathon race is usually 50 kilometres, increasing to multi-day events (such as ours) and trans-country / trans-continent runs, and even beyond. To run a standard marathon successfully requires a degree of physical training. To run an ultra-marathon successfully requires a high degree of physical conditioning and mental preparation. The differences between marathon and ultra had influenced my method of training program when I finally got my act together, and at the start of December 2005 I signed up to the 'Mad Dog Training Team'. I now had an on-line coach – Mike 'Mad Dog' Schreiber, who is an ultra-distance runner based in Mexico, and who provides personalized training programs for any runner wanting to improve at any distance from complete beginner to multi-day ultra-runner.

Andrea had given birth to our son, William, on 4th December 2005. With increased family responsibility as well as a full time job and university work, training time was now at its most limited. Every minute had to count. I had exchanged a few emails with Mad Dog earlier in the year as he answers general training queries free of charge, and he was aware of our plans to run the coast-to-coast. When I joined his team the first thing he did was to give me a reprimand regarding having got myself injured and not having signed up sooner – the latter would have prevented the former! Mad Dog asked me for my recent running history as well as general information such as age, height, weight etc. and details of my injury and rehab program. His first task was to get me running properly again, something I had done little of since trying to shred my Achilles with the sprints up the dam wall nearly three months previously. Mad Dog emailed a weekly schedule describing distances and pacing to be run, broken down into daily and weekly totals. Far greater use was made of my available time. I was to run no more than four times per week; a long weekend run and, in the week, two short fast runs and a hill session. The weekly total mileage started considerably lower than prior to my injury. This initially frustrated me, thinking 'I can run farther than this, so surely I *should* be running farther'. I was falling for the quality verses quantity trap again. The hill sessions were turned completely on their head compared with what I had been doing. My idea of hill training was to run uphill fast at lung bursting speed then jog slowly back down to recover before repeating. Wrong! To run a multi-day ultra I would have to conserve as much energy going uphill as possible then avoid fighting gravity on the downhill. My instructions for the hill sessions were "uphill slow and real easy, flat sections comfortable, downhill flying!" The short fast runs were to start at moderate pace and gradually speed up until I was finishing with a sprint. Weekend long runs were to be at a steady pace with the second half faster than the first, and were immediately followed by a jog/walk period where I would walk for a minute then jog slowly for a minute and repeat.

Added to this were a number of exercises that had to be done immediately following each run, and also done at home at anytime. He advised I buy some ankle weights and wear them as much as possible. This I did, causing some intrigue at work for the first few weeks until my colleagues became used to them. For some of the runs I wore them round my wrists to increase the effort required to haul my body round the course, and give my upper body a workout with the pumping action of my weighted arms. I was also to put weights in my Camelbak and wear it as much as possible, whether running or not, to become accustomed to carrying the load. The rationale was to make every waking hour some form of physical training. With William's arrival many of my waking hours were nocturnal, and even these could be utilised for training. Whilst holding him following a night feed I'd do some leg exercises such as partial squats, combining winding the baby with weight training.

The first weekly schedule from Mad Dog seemed ludicrously easy: -

6(+), 0, 3, 0, 5, 3, 0 = 17 Plus 5 minutes jog/walk.

That meant six miles steady running on Sunday followed immediately by five minutes of the jog/walk cycle, three miles fast on Tuesday and Friday and five miles of hills on Thursday, making a weekly total of only seventeen miles. I was used to three or four times that amount. However he was the expert and I was the injured fool and I wisely put myself in his hands and followed everything he said.

The first few runs caused a little pain in the Achilles area but Mick the physio had told me to expect this and, as long as it didn't worsen, to carry on. Within a few days I was running the short distances pain free. Over the weeks the weekly totals gradually increased, one week the long run would lengthen, the next, one of the speed sessions, then the hill session. Then there would be a week of decreased distance before another progressive increase. With such a busy home life it was far better to have all the thinking taken out of my training (not that I thought about it much before!) and to know what was expected days in advance. A great effort was made to minimise the impact of my running on the rest of my family. I found that if I prepared sandwiches in advance I had time in my work's lunch break to do the speed session, have a strip wash and gulp down lunch before returning to work in the afternoon. I even managed to do this when the distances had increased to seven miles of speed work as I'd got quite fast by then. I'd arrange my shifts so that I finished early on Thursdays to do the hills before Andrea brought Hannah home from nursery. On Sundays I'd wake early and run before anyone else got up. Or better still if we were to go to relatives for Sunday lunch I'd either run there or run home after.

By the end of the coast-to-coast training my schedule was more like: -

20(+), 0, 7, 0, 12, 7, 0 = 46 (plus 1:45 jog/walk). Two seven mile fast runs at lunchtime, twelve miles of hills on Thursday evening and twenty miles of running and another eight or so of jog/walking on Sunday. Most of the runs involved wearing the backpack, which contained weight equivalent to that I expected to carry on the coast-to-coast. I was encouraged to enter some road races to add spice to the regime, and wore the weighted backpack for these as well. The first was the Dronfield 10K road race. Warming up beforehand and at the start of this event I felt self-conscious as I was, not surprisingly, the only runner with a backpack, getting several peculiar looks from some of the other competitors. I ran well, passing people throughout the entire hilly run and finishing within a minute of my personal best time for the distance. Stopping only briefly to collect my finisher's medal I went straight into 90 minutes of the jog/walk program, still carrying the backpack.

The next race was the Sheffield Lord Mayor's 10K that started and finished in the Don Valley Stadium. Following the good run at Dronfield I was proud of running with the backpack, confident that I could beat most of the field even when carrying weights. This was an even better performance, knocking over a minute off my personal best. And immediately after the run I scheduled a two-hour jog/walk, which I used to get myself back home. I doubt many people that day ran a personal best carrying a weighted rucksack, then did ten miles back home on foot. Evidently Mad Dog's training program was working, and working well.

I had never actually spoken to Mad Dog, only ever conversing via email, but I think we started to know each other pretty well. He described himself as "very old, with lots of hair", and said that he had been running ultra-distance trail races for over 50 years. Some of his stories from previous events were hilarious. With a friend he used to train running through the streets of Houston wearing altitude simulators. People thought they were astronauts in training, or heart patients. Over the weeks I found out some of his past in the US military, and that he lives in the mountains in Mexico and runs with his Dalmatian dog called Sparkey. He taught me many things including what a 'Foo Fighter' was (not the rock band), and that ultra-running had nothing to do with sanity and everything to do with carrying on regardless.

My speed continued to increase, and during some of the subsequent lunchtime runs I knocked a few more minutes off my 10k best time, eventually getting it down to 37 minutes

The non-running training was also going extremely well. I was able to do pretty much unlimited numbers of partial squats, which made my quad (thigh) muscles bomb-proof, and was wearing the leg weights constantly. Most evenings I did sets of press-ups and crunches. The Camelbak was rarely off my back out of the workplace, and domestic chores saw me sporting ankle weights, wrist weights and the backpack.

Mad Dog had also been preparing me mentally. He claimed that for ultra running the brain was the most important organ in the body. Not only did I know how to pace myself, but also I had developed a belief that I was not going to fail. No matter what! My long distance training had regularly involved discomfort and pain (I was covering a marathon distance most Sundays, and running flat out for seven miles at a time twice weekly) and had developed ways to minimise it or become accustomed to it. I was ready both physically and mentally to run ultra-marathons.

oooOooo

Even standing on the roadside in Reeth in the grey drizzly morning after having run 96 miles and with a very stiff knee stinging with every step, I still had absolute belief that I would not fail. The weather was far from ideal with low cloud hanging in the valley, hugging Swale, and constant drizzle penetrated the grey gloominess. Justin was on the bike team for another day. A day that promised to be as demanding mentally as physically, not only due to the very long distance to be travelled but also because the greater part would be flat, dull and generally unstimulating. Before us lay the Vale of York, a low-lying wide valley that was created by glaciers as they retreated over Triassic sandstone and Jurassic mudstone at the end of the last ice age. Generally flat, bar one or two ridges that were formed by glacial moraine, the Vale would offer little in the way of visual or navigational challenge. The leaden skies and misty drizzle compounded the lack of stimulus, promising six hours or so of little to focus on but the physical and mental pains of a tortured day's running. Vin stretched against the wall of the stone outbuilding next to me whilst Justin and Mal prepared their bikes. The rain bounced back up to ankle level as it hit the ground, before filling the innumerable puddles and running into little streams that flowed down the road out of Reeth to the east, the way we would go. We had made plans to preserve our injured limbs and hopefully minimise the pain. The initial route, which involved roughly 50% off-road running, had been changed to make it completely on tarmac, as this made for smoother travel and less twisting strain on the joints, although a trade-off was an increase in the pounding impact with each step. There would also be a decrease in the mental stimulus required, as navigation would be much simpler. Vin was worried about his thigh and wanted to walk the first mile before attempting to run. I suspected he was more worried than he was letting on when he set off alone without the usual team backslapping and good-luck wishing. I finished assisting Andy loading my bag into the roof box and set off after Vin at a gentle jog, catching him a couple of hundred yards out of Reeth. From behind he looked very lithe and athletic in his Lycra leggings and tight long-sleeved running shirt as he power-walked. His slim Camelbak rucksack helped to give the impression that he'd been stretched upwards and that he should really be shorter and wider. We were both dressed for the cooler damp weather, I also wore jogging trousers and had arm warmers on as well as a running T-shirt underneath a thin rain jacket. The road swung gently to the right and we crossed Swale on an attractive stone bridge at the small village of Grinton. From above I looked down at the water and it smiled back through a surface roughed and rippled by the incessant deluge. Then an immediate sharp left turn ensured we still traveled with the river, but now observing it from across its flood plain on the right bank, something we had only done for half a mile at the mouth of Whitsundale Beck. At the one-mile point Vin steadily upped the pace and started a gentle jog. I stayed on his shoulder, letting him dictate how fast we went, suffering a little with my knee. A shout from behind heralded the arrival and passing of the two bikers, rain jackets flapping, back wheels spraying a Mohican of road dirt up into the air and striping their backs as they whizzed easily past. Justin was riding several yards behind Mal, and looked a little more uncomfortable as if trying not to let the gap between them widen. This would be a relatively easy day for the two of them physically, but also unstimulating with the absence of any significant hills. The slightest hint of a downhill slope came and Vin was immediately limping. Within 50 yards he was walking again. My knee niggled but was no worse when running than walking. He attempted to run again but soon pulled back to a walk. His pace was too fast for me to walk yet slower than my jog and several times I found myself dropping back some distance before jogging to catch him up. We'd gone less than two miles and it was already a major ordeal. Continuing at this pace we'd be jog/walking for over nine hours to get to Ingleby Cross, a prospect I didn't find appealing. We stopped by a gateway into a field to water the hedgerow and review our options. A decision was made to stay together until the four-mile mark, which represented a total of 100 miles traveled since leaving St Bees. After that I would run on ahead and leave my limping companion to power walk as best as he could. Wisely Vin had taken a spare set of the day's maps from Mal so we were both able to navigate alone. And alone we would probably be, as we hadn't arranged any rendezvous points with Andy and the support car. Not only that, such was the lack of coherent team thinking during the morning's preparation we'd neglected Orff and forgotten to play *Carmina Burana*. As usual we each carried a radio but these only had a range of three miles so the likelihood was that most of the day we would be out of contact with each other.

The four mile point arrived as the road entered a wooded section between Reeth and Richmond. Vin was still unable to run and had given up trying. We wished each other good luck, had a manly embrace, patted each other on the back, and I broke into a jog. Thankfully this was still no more painful than walking and I was relieved at the prospect of cutting three hours off the day's travelling time – assuming I made it! I was now alone, heading for Richmond, the largest town on the coast-to-coast route. The town was founded by the Normans in 1071 and grew up around the castle built on the 'Riche-Mont', meaning Strong Hill. Its history as a settlement goes way beyond that, however. Flints shaped for hunting and tool making dating back to the Neolithic period (4000 – 2000 BC) were excavated nearby. Remains of Iron Age fortifications have also been found. The Romans inhabited the area, and as they gradually withdrew to other parts of their empire (after doing their bit in the pillage of Gunnerside), Anglo-Saxon invaders, then later Danes and Norsemen, landed. The Danes turned to arable farming in the lowlands whilst the Norse kept to uplands farming, grazing sheep and cattle, and each provided the origins of local place names such as Skeeby, Thwaite, Muker and Applegarth. Christianity later came to the area when the monk Paulinus baptised Edwin, King of Northumbria. Hundreds of people were later baptised in the River Swale at a point near Catterick, which became known as The Holy River and the Jordan of England.

The journey to Richmond, only ten miles or so from Reeth, was an ordeal. Five miles per hour seemed to be my maximum pace as numerous walk breaks were required. The pages on the map were being turned far more slowly than I had anticipated. I was ticking off natural and man-made geographical features as I ran; caravan parks, stream crossings, bends in the road, and time appeared to slow down between each one. Just after our parting company the road contoured round a little stream and doubled back on itself in a deep 'U' shape at 'Eddy's Bridge'. Although often looking behind me I was not able to see Vin following on the other side of the bend, but surely he couldn't have been that far behind? Another mile and the B6270 joined the much busier A6108. Now it was horrible, running along a major road into a regional town, with no footpath, water laden bushes and trees overhanging and sagging into my way, vehicles thundering past spraying grimy water into the air. Like the end of the previous day's efforts I was forced to hug the hedgerow simply to survive. Perhaps we should have taken our chances with the off-road route after all, or better still jumped in Swale and floated with her as she eased herself effortlessly down the valley. Drowning in a beautiful river would be preferable to being taken out by the meteorite impact of a rampaging HGV. I crossed the river again at Lownethwaite Bridge, and here Swale looked more excitable from up on the high span. The water rushed over shallows and rocks as if hurrying me along into the town, the outskirts of which I was now reaching.

Two hours after starting the day I entered Richmond, which on a late Saturday morning was a busy bustling town with what seemed like far too many cars and people, all hustling and moving erratically and generally getting in the way of my straight running line. One car slowed to my speed as it came alongside, the window dropped down and a familiar voice asked me how I was doing. Andy, who was last away from the bed and breakfast, met Vin still limping along the A6108 and left him about a mile or two behind me. He wanted to know if I needed anything. With a gesture of my right arm I directed him to park on the next side street so I could get some supplies. Without my running partner I needed another distraction to take my mind off the long dull painful ordeal. Andy opened the roof box and after a short rummage in my kit bag I was able to pull out my MP3 player, and pushed it into the top of my Camelbak. Whilst I ate some scrummy I was pleased to hear Andy inform me that Vin was still battling on, albeit slowly. I was pretty sure he wouldn't give in.

The small hill down out of Richmond, Anchorage Hill, which passes by the gates of St Trinnian's Hall, was the last notable gradient for the day, and I ran this section fast, wondering whether the Hall had any connection with the fictional girls' school that was created by the British cartoonist Ronald Searle. The school is the antithesis of the Enid Blyton-type posh girls boarding school in that the pupils are badly behaved and often armed with hockey sticks and catapults, and the teachers equally disreputable. The girls often drank, gambled and smoke, and many fell victim to violence in the form of anarchic team sports. No nubile young women in gym-slip style dress screamed at me or threatened to give chase and offer a hockey stick beating as I passed the gates of the Hall. And that was hugely disappointing. But not surprising as not only is the school fictional but I later discovered that St Trinian's school is named after St Trinnean's in Edinburgh, several hundred miles to the north. Being chased by a marauding gang of schoolgirls would, however, have been the perfect distraction as from here on it was flat, flat, flat for the rest of the day. I made the decision to keep my music machine in my backpack for as long as I could, only to use it as pain relief when absolutely needed. Approaching the crossing of the immensely busy A1 road at Brompton-on-Swale I could hear the roar of *infernal* combustion engines, growling along the road like a giant predator, intent on savaging me to a painful violent death. The noise as I entered the underpass felt like I was being assaulted, and I was spurred to run faster to escape the savagery. Little by little the din faded as I plodded east and the suburban landscape gave way to mile after mile of identical arable farmland, punctuated only by the occasional tiny village. Just before one such village, Scorton, I saw a walkers' signpost labeled 'C2C', pointing off the road towards Swale, which was still to my right hand side following the river crossing just before Richmond. Checking on the map, a small dotted green line could be seen passing through a bare area of chart on which was written "Sand and Gravel Pit". The path appeared to cut a corner of the road and head towards Bolton-on-Swale. Worth a look, I thought, and pushed the metal gate open before heading quickly down a slight grassy incline toward the riverbank, listening for the clang as the gate swung shut behind me. By the river the path turned left and promptly disappeared, or so it seemed, into the gravel pits. I wasn't prepared to spend valuable time getting lost chasing non-existent trails through dug-up ground, so turned round and retraced my steps back to the road. Hearing the gate clang shut behind me for a second time I strangely felt a sense of disappointment and was unsure why. Was it because I had just wasted a few minutes taking an unsuccessful unplanned detour, or maybe because I'd chosen an easier navigational option rather than testing my skills traversing the gravel pits? On reaching Scorton I checked the map again and I had a third theory. The 'C2C' sign I had seen directed me to Swale at the point the river turned southwards, whilst I would be continuing east. That had been our parting, the last point I would see my friend Swale, my silent companion with whom I had meandered for the last two days. Swale knew it but I hadn't realised, and she tempted me with the sign and pulled me over to her bank one final time. She had gone and I never said goodbye.

Now bored by the long, lonely dull plod along unremarkable lanes, and developing a general whole body ache to accompany the knee pain, I decided on the village of Bolton-on-Swale two miles away as the point at which I would succumb to musical distraction. For an extra treat I also planned to eat a sports energy bar there. Oh, the excitement, the anticipation! Things were that desperate! As I lumbered along, having already been running alone for three hours, I yearned away the distance to my 'bonus'. I was certain that the music would raise my flagging spirits, reduce the pain and give my running speed an uplifting boost.

One mile to go and I could have some 'rock and roll' to numb the aching.

Half a mile and the thumping rhythms would drag me from the malaise into which I was slipping. And there was the promise of the energy bar. Bolton-on-Swale couldn't come soon enough.

At last! I turned left off the main road into the village and reached the church. My salvation. The church symbol on the map represented my finishing line of dullness and the start of a new musically enhanced spell of enlightened running, all the way to Ingleby Cross still nearly twenty miles away. Still running, I slid the pack off my shoulders and fumbled around in the small outer pocket, feeling for my treasure. The wires connecting the earpieces to the small unit were quickly located and I dragged them out, swapping hands so I could feel around for the energy bar. This had slipped right to the bottom of the pocket, from where I dragged it before holding it in my teeth, still in its wrapper. Bubbling, hissing noises accompanied my journey as I panted and wheezed heavily with the wrapper in my mouth, still running, trying to reposition the Camelbak without dropping the MP3. Backpack on, I carefully inserted each earpiece, put the supporting cord round my neck and switched the unit on.

Nothing!

I pressed the on switch again.

Nothing!

Another press.

Still nothing!

Flat battery!

I felt a huge sense of disappointment and attempted to swear, but having the energy bar held in my teeth and breathing heavily from running, all that came out was a frustrated hissing "Basshdassh!" Frustration soon gave way to a philosophical acceptance that this ultra-marathon business wasn't supposed to be easy and I was just going to have to accept the suffering and dig deeper into mental reserves. The MP3 was unceremoniously stuffed back into the pocket with the wrapper of the energy bar. As I chewed and jogged I casually surveyed the landscape around me. Where was I, or more importantly where was everyone else? I appeared to have stumbled into some strange world, a place containing all the artefacts and trappings of rural existence, but deserted, recently abandoned of human existence. To the left stood a large cluster of farm buildings, well-maintained and standing watch over fields of healthy looking crops that gently danced in the light teasing breeze, but no evidence of a farmer. No farm dog barking at me as I ran past the driveway. No activity. Ahead and a little to the right were a couple of immaculate looking brick-built houses, one with washing hanging neatly on a rotary airer (in this weather?), but no occupants visible, nobody out tending the cared-for gardens. There were no cars meandering along the lanes. Come to think of it, despite it being Saturday I hadn't seen a soul for quite some time. Farms but no farmers, houses but no people, roads but nothing travelling on them! Where was everybody? Apart from the sounds of nature, which was doing its best attempt at hushed quiet, there was silence. A deep silence in which, if I listened hard enough, I could hear the pounding of my overworked heart trying to burst through my rib cage and scuttle away to hide. I felt quite alone, contemplating some conspiracy theory with me the victim. Was this my own *Truman Show* and the cast had left the set, leaving me in my own private universe of illusions? If so, the special effects team had thankfully left the rain machine off, at least for now. With no obvious way out of this reality and into a more comfortable one, I ran on towards Whitwell.

Throughout the course of a very long run both body and mind undergo cyclic changes, increases and decreases in performance and tolerance to the extreme physical events. Periods of near euphoria and abundant strength are followed by a sense of gloom and heightened awareness that every muscle, joint and sinew is being pounded and traumatised into pointless agony. An air of invincibility quickly converts to a belief that failure is inevitable and to continue will be folly. Despite the disappointment of the music machine, the snack seemed to swing the cycle upwards once again, probably aided by the rain having stopped, and I was moving well, studying the map for potential route changes off the roads. There was an option of a bridleway, not shorter in distance than the tarmac option, but off-road and therefore a change for flesh and soul. On reaching the gate at the roadside, the trail I was to take surprised me, though it shouldn't have. Having run the previous days mostly over rocky hills and firm grassland, seeing a path running through the edge of a field of crops, saturated by the rain, was somehow bizarrely disconcerting. I should have expected this, surrounded as I was by arable farms, but clearly I wasn't thinking straight. Knee-high wet crops would soak my legs and feet. I'd get water in my running shoes. That can't happen! Should I turn back and run an extra mile to rejoin the original route. How could it all have gone so horribly wrong? I was either in the throes of a bonk or five days of consecutive marathon running was messing with my cerebral synapses.

Thankfully, rational thought took over before I sat down by the gate to wait indefinitely for nothing. Wet legs and feet! What was all the winter training for, or any of the training for that matter? Why, after running for hours in the rain, was I upset at the thought of crossing this field? Mad Dog had previously informed me that an ultra-distance runner's most important weapon was the brain. Right now my most important weapon evidently needed sharpening. With a slap across the face, I laughed at the irrationality of it and set off down the bridleway. Within twenty yards my legs were indeed soaking wet and there was water in my shoes, but it was refreshing, and I was curiously delighted to see my shoes brushed clean of the accumulated grime and looking like they had just been taken out of the box.

But apart from the mental shenanigans, the day was still mostly dull. Through the gate at the far side of the field I disturbed a fox, rooting through the hedgerow. It turned and fled 30 yards before standing, staring at me from the centre of a recently ploughed field. I stared back. It stared harder. A game! Something to do, a challenge! Disappointingly the fox wasn't as interested in our standoff, and nonchalantly turned and meandered slowly away, heading towards Hodber Hill Plantation.

Back on winding country lanes the mental carousel gradually turned back to the dark side. Although not actually lost I felt to be in the middle of nowhere, going nowhere, whole body aching, knee stinging, no end in sight. Short periods of walking became more common and I had to stop completely and stretch to loosen a stiff aching back. I halted under the canopy of a willow tree, where the road was drier. A hundred metres to my left a group of boys in their early teens played a rowdy game of football in a field containing several tents pitched in a semicircle. At the centre of the arc stood a flag pole that was constructed from lengths of wood lashed together with twine, and that had a casual, almost intentional bend to one side as if trying gently to lower the heavy rain-soaked union flag to the ground rather than drop it unceremoniously. Having spent several weeks at scout camps in my youth I recognized the signs of one immediately. This was life at its most enthusiastic. *The Truman Show* must have been back on air, but I felt too stiff and aching to take a leading role. Dropping my Camelbak from my shoulders I awkwardly got to the ground and lay in the road, staring upward through the dangling branches at nothing in particular in the grey nothingness beyond. It was drizzling lightly again. A weeping sky through the weeping willow! I closed my eyes and felt a dull ache just about everywhere, but not to be moving was nice, very nice. I stretched my back, then lay there a bit longer. Then a bit longer still. With pained effort I stood up again, worried that the scouts would come over and jump up and down on my chest in an enthusiastic attempt at resuscitation, before dragging me off to their camp by the ging-gang-goolies. Or worse, some kamikaze farmer in his Massey-Ferguson would bounce along the lane and run over me, leaving me wedged in one of the wheel arches with the rest of the farm slurry. One foot in front of the other, off again.

Another featureless grey lane, and now I was out of drink. Looking up the road I wished the crew car to be just round a right hand bend that was a hundred yards away. Within ten seconds of my wish I had to step to the side of the lane to let a car come past. Only it didn't pass, it pulled alongside and the driver asked if I wanted anything. Andy had evidently developed psychic powers! Unbelievable! How on earth had they found me on the maze of crisscrossing lanes and farm tracks that sat on the map like an old tangled fishing net? How did they find me at exactly the moment I wished for them? Perhaps it was Justin's excellent navigational skills, predicting the route I'd take and searching along it. But when I looked at the person in the passenger seat it wasn't Justin, it was Vin.

oooOooo

With hindsight, the vision of Vin sitting in the car shouldn't have been a surprise, but it was. I truly believed that, despite his slow painful progress, he would grind out the journey to Ingleby Cross before merrily planning the next day's outing during the evening meal. However, on the approach to Richmond, Vin's thigh had worsened dramatically. Andy had left him hobbling along the A6108 but at least still moving, and with a pain level that was tolerable though unpleasant. The next mile changed things, and by the time he reached the town he was unable to walk. On more than one occasion passing motorists had stopped to ask if he was OK. He'd told them he was, but wasn't. Inevitability took over. There was no possibility of his continuing another 23 miles so he stopped in Richmond and telephoned Andy to pick him up. His running of the coast-to-coast was over. Thankfully I had been unaware of these events, as the news of his inability to continue had resulted in the rest of the team feeling deflated. Had I been informed of Vin's demise during a psychologically difficult period I may have felt less inclined to press on. Surprisingly he appeared quite philosophical and buoyant as I chatted to him while we stood behind the crew car. I didn't want to ask him too much about it in case he was trying to hide disappointment; I knew I would have been distraught at dropping out after all the preparation and training. I felt a confusing cocktail of emotions; honest disappointment for my running colleague's misfortune, trepidation at the prospect of running, and navigating, the rest of the way alone, but also a guilty and perverse sense of victory. For the first time ever, I had beaten Vin, I had won a battle of attrition! But of course this wasn't true, just my human nature clutching at shreds of an imagined victory. We were a team, and he was the stronger member. If we had been competing against each other from the start, he would probably have already been at Ingleby Cross waiting for me to stumble along. However, this wasn't the time to reflect. I had to re-focus and press ahead.

The first thing I asked for was a new battery for my MP3 player, which was promptly supplied, then some pain killers before refuelling began, both food for myself and drink for my reservoir. The rain had abated but a chilly wind blew and, whilst I was warm from the physical effort, my colleagues shivered as they attended to my hunger, Vin being particularly cold as he was yet to change out of his damp running clothes. The offer of a hot cup of tea was refused, as it would have taken longer than I wanted to stop to boil the kettle on the portable stove. Both team-mates wished me good luck and watched me set off again. No time was wasted in starting up the MP3 player, and the volume was turned up as loud as possible without risking not hearing approaching traffic or my communications radio. The first track fired me up – Vertigo by *U2*. I had regularly listened to this CD many times whilst mentally preparing for the run and it instantly gave me a kick up the backside. Combined with the food intake and a fresh pack full of drink (and probably the painkillers) I was back on a high, making good progress and singing along as the crew car passed by heading to meet the riders at the B+B. The lyrics of the next few songs were a powerful support to my mental stubbornness. I passed through the village of Streetlam and then the rain started again in earnest as I approached Danby Wiske. *U2* had finished and been replaced by *REM* by the time I crossed the A167 at Oaktree Hill and joined another bridleway, passing two walkers who were sheltering under a large tree. Both were clothed head to ankle in thick waterproofs with the hoods pulled tight around their faces, and both wore expressions of miserable damp discomfort. The energy boost I'd felt from the pit stop was wearing off and it was again getting tough, although I forced myself to keep running through the 26 mile marathon distance to ensure I passed that mark within five hours. Considering the very slow start to the day and also that it was the fifth consecutive day's marathon I was pleased with the time, but I was definitely sinking into another low period. Heading up a slight incline towards the village of Deighton my radio sparked into life. I pulled the MP3 earplugs out and lifted the radio from my pack to hear more clearly. It was Mal's voice.

"Matty, are you there?"

"Helloooooo," I replied.

"Matty, where are you?"

"Heading towards Deighton, just south of it."

"I guess we'll see you in a minute or so then."

Almost immediately the car appeared round a left hand bend. Andy was driving, with Mal in the passenger seat and Justin in the back with the big video camera and surrounded by mess and rubbish, empty drinks cans, sweet wrappers, rummaged-through bags and other flotsam and jetsam that the crew had accumulated since leaving St Bees. I was delighted that, after unpacking their bags at the bed and breakfast, the three of them had decided to search me out and give me much needed support. I was OK for supplies, the support they came to bring was psychological - telling me how great I was doing and not to stop – and this made me feel quite emotional. They didn't want to put me in the car and take me to Ingleby Cross, they wanted to cheer me as I pounded the route all the way there. Mal offered me a can of Red Bull, which I downed while Justin filmed and asked a couple of questions.

"How far have you gone so far?" I checked the GPS. It read 27½ miles. Six miles to go! That's just about 10K. A normal lunchtime run would see that covered in less than 40 minutes. Not today!

Mal studied my map, and pointing announced, "We'll see you again there!" This was fantastic, superb support. I set off again, hearing the noise of the car turning round behind me. As they passed Mal and Andy applauded and cheered whilst Justin filmed from the back seat. I was riding on a wave of euphoria. The hills immediately behind Ingleby Cross, although shrouded in mist, were now clearly visible on the near horizon. Suddenly they didn't seem far, and furthermore I had another rendezvous point in three miles. I turned up the music and ran.

East of Deighton the road passed over a railway line at a level crossing. Fortunately no trains were coming so my steady running was unimpeded. Merrily singing along to the music, I pulled a bag of jelly sweets from my pack and chewed on three or four in a calculated effort to maintain blood sugar levels. This was something I tried to remember to do every hour or so. Too few jellies and I'd bonk. Too many and I'd give myself a sugar rush followed by an equally debilitating bonk. It was a fine line to tread. I could see the crew car from half a mile away, waiting where I was scheduled to leave the road for the last bridleway section. As I approached Mal stepped out and handed another can of Red Bull. This time I didn't stop, just waved to the other guys in the car and drank the stimulant drink as I ran along the farm track. A very short but steep crossing of a stream valley reduced me to a walk, there being little strength left in my legs for hills. Round a series of 90-degree bends in the track Mal was again waiting for me, clutching another can of Red Bull. *REM* had finished and *Stone Roses*, one of Mal's favourite bands, were now powering me along. I pulled one earpiece out to listen to him as he ran alongside. My right ear enjoyed 'She Bangs the Drum' whilst my left listened to him announce that he had come to escort me across the very busy A19 road. When he and Justin had arrived there on their bikes they had to wait several minutes for a safe gap to hurry across, and he felt that after 33 miles of running I might require assistance to get over safely. Luck was on my side, as a very small break in the traffic occurred as I reached the hard shoulder, and I was able to sprint across, hardly breaking stride, with Mal beside me. Mal was amazed by the crossing, and likened me to the character Morpheus in the film *The Matrix* - the speeding cars appearing to bend around me as if they were mere works of mental trickery. Then he reminded himself yet again to always wear the correct footwear, his feet now aching due to running alongside me in his rigid-soled biking shoes.

The crew car was parked directly opposite on the edge of the side road that led to the day's destination, windows down with Justin filming and Andy talking on his mobile phone. Mal pointed down the side road and informed me that there was less than half a mile to go down an easy descent. Again they turned and drove past me, but pulled up half way down the hill where Vin was standing with my camera. He fired off a few shots of my arrival before we exchanged high-fives as I ran past, not stopping until I reached the bed and breakfast at the bottom. Everything hurt, but I was high on endorphins and a sense of achievement and the pain was vastly less than it had been before they found me at Deighton. I stopped the timer on the GPS and read the details – 33 miles in five hours 58 minutes. I stood alone for only ten seconds or so before the team arrived with their congratulations. The boot was opened and once again the reliable Justin was forthcoming with sustenance.

The phone call Andy was taking as I crossed the A19 was from Andrea, asking how we were doing. He was just telling her about my imminent approach and asked if she wanted to speak to me. She said not, instead instructing him to shout me to "keep going", which he had done as I passed. Even Andrea didn't want me to stop.

The bed and breakfast was small and simple but comfortable enough, situated at the base of Arncliffe Wood. The view out of the window looked up towards the hills of the North York Moors, upon which the low clouds hung like a tattered old blanket, and where, body willing, I'd be running tomorrow. Inside the doorway to Andy's room a parcel was waiting that contained two more cases of Red Bull that had been posted on to us. After the usual shower and cold soak I laid on my bed and watched Liverpool football club win the FA cup, disturbed only by the entry of Vin who wished to talk to Justin with whom I again shared a room. Although unable to run, Vin had a plan.

Outside in the street the shoes fitted, the bike felt right and even Justin's helmet was the right size for Vin as he cycled back and forth along the lane, testing his leg. His idea was feasible! OK, so running the full length of the coast to coast had proven unsuccessful, but by borrowing Justin's cycling gear he could still make the full distance under his own power. Following breakfast the next morning the plan was for Andy to drive Vin and the bike back to Richmond to the point he'd dropped out of the run, and Vin would ride back to Ingleby Cross before continuing on roads to Day 6 destination at Glaisdale. If that proved successful he'd reassess the situation regarding his leg and decide whether to run or bike the final stage to the finish. The idea lifted the spirits of the whole team to see one of the athletes back on track, albeit by a different mode of transport. Maps were studied in the pub during evening meal and, although charts for the road ride from Ingleby Cross to Glaisdale weren't available, rough directions were written for Vin to follow.

The evening meal was disappointing – the worst we'd experienced so far on our adventure, but it was edible. Just! No fine home cooked fare here, this was mass produced, pre-packaged additive-laden rubbish, not lovingly cooked but given a whirlwind two-minute tour round the inside of a microwave oven. Totally exhausted from the day's efforts, I didn't know whether to eat it or let my head fall in it and drift away into slumberous oblivion. I barely made it awake to the end of the meal before heading to bed and crashing straight to sleep.

oooOooo

Solo

Day 6. Sunday 14th May 2006. Ingleby Cross to Glaisdale.
26.5 miles

We were all up for an early breakfast, wanting to get off to a good start. Andy needed to get Vin back to Richmond, while Mal and I would be heading up onto the Moors. At least that's what I intended if I could get my knee to move with only a reasonable amount of pain. It hurt a lot, and it was the type of hurt that was telling me to stop running immediately. Under normal circumstances I would have stopped at Keld some 50 miles back, if not before. But these were not normal circumstances. The coast-to-coast was my Olympics, my World Cup, almost my *raison d'être* for the last few months. Motivation, training, and blind stubbornness fired me to put on my running kit again and spend a long time performing stretches to increase flexibility and hopefully reduce pain. The thought of the money we were attempting to raise for charity had only a little bearing on attempting to continue; it was mainly my own bloody-mindedness at getting through this one-off event. "No permanent damage," I kept telling myself, "just don't do any permanent damage".

he charity aspect had materialised late on in the organisational proceedings. Many people had enquired whether we were doing the event for charity, and we eventually tired of explaining that it was all for our own pleasure. The idea of running 180 miles being quite extreme, most people we knew were more than happy to sponsor the effort, and we finally chose the Children In Need charity to benefit as we had run the night marathon in their aid. A link to the charity was immediately put on our web site, a site that had been developed by Andy. This had been an extra source of entertainment for us all – writing our individual profiles, devising 'rules of engagement', posting images in a 'photo album', and writing regular updates. The name of the web site was taken from a comment by Mal that somehow summed up what we were attempting – www.respectthestupidity.com

The site went 'live' on March 27th 2006, approximately six weeks before we were to start the event, and hits were received immediately as we told friends and family about the site. Each evening during the coast-to-coast a brief update was written from each aspect – running, biking or crew – and posted on the site for followers to view our progress.

The first significant event to go on the 'latest update' section prior to our leaving for Cumbria was an ankle injury Vin sustained with only a month or so to go, twisting it badly during a fast training run. It immediately ballooned in size and turned purple, and he was unable to walk. This was almost identical to an injury he suffered a couple of years before, on that occasion taking over three months to recover. This time he didn't have three months. But he did make it to the start, as did I, also with my injured ankle. Yet it wasn't his ankle that caused his drop out from the running, or mine that threatened failure almost within sight of the coast.

oooOooo

Despite his assurances that he felt fine about the move to biking, Vin looked somewhat forlorn sitting in the passenger seat of the car as Andy set off with him back to Richmond, waved off by Mal and myself who were standing outside our accommodation and ready to go. Justin filmed their departure before turning the camera onto us as we set off together towards the steep slopes that stood in our way, now clearly seen as the damp low cloud had receded overnight into a general cool greyness. The gradients on the initially planned route for Day 6 were severe, up onto the Cleveland Hills near Osmotherly, followed by several sharp climbs and descents along the edge of an escarpment in an east-north-easterly direction. A last minute change saw us choosing a less painful route southeasterly up the flatter valley of Scugdale before turning east onto the moors.

The geology of the North York Moors is dominated by rocks of the Jurassic age that were mostly laid down in tropical seas 205 to 142 million years ago. Fluctuations in sea level produced different rock types varying from shales to sandstones and limestones formed from coral. These deposited rocks are superbly exposed on the Yorkshire coast from Staithes to Filey, and contain a myriad of fossils, evidence of the dinosaurs and other creatures that roamed and swam the area. Subsequently, about 30 million years ago, the land was lifted and tilted towards the south by earth movements. The upper layers of rock were eroded away and the older rocks exposed in places. As a result of the tilt the oldest rocks in the north became exposed. These are bands of shales and ironstones forming the steep terrain on the northern scarp of the moors and Cleveland Hills, which stand high and proud, looming over the Vale we had traversed so arduously yesterday. The middle layers form the sandstones of the high moors, which we were hoping to cross without incident, and the youngest layers of limestone form the hills to the south. In the most recent glacial period, which ended around 20,000 years ago, the higher parts of the North York Moors were not covered by the ice sheets but glaciers flowed southwards on either side of the higher land mass. As the climate became warmer and the snowfields on the moors began to melt the water was unable to escape northwards, westwards or eastwards as it was still blocked by ice. Vast torrents of water flowed southwards, gouging out Newtondale valley as it went, and forming a vast lake in the area of the Vale of Pickering. These geological processes left an area of high moorland towering steeply over flat valleys to the north, west and south, and standing guard over the North Sea to the east, an area of natural beauty, outstanding in every sense of the word. Aelred, the Abbot of Rievaulx Abbey (1142-1167), summed the North Yorkshire Moors up thus: "Everywhere peace, everywhere serenity, and a marvellous freedom from the tumult of the world." I didn't know it but my tumult was about to worsen.

It was to be a difficult day for the support crew, with three athletes spread over a wide area, although Vin would be left mainly to his own devices. Fortunately his mother, Ans, was well on her way up from Kent up to see him and give us support, and he was in mobile phone contact with her. Justin had to wait at the B+B for Andy's return before loading our bags into the car and heading for our first rendezvous of the day at Seave Green.

As soon as we set off I was in trouble. My legs felt quite strong but the knee pain was constant and worse than it had been on previous days, and I struggled to keep the pace around eleven minutes per mile even on flat roads. Mal and I chatted, wondering how Vin would manage if he needed an urgent toilet stop whilst biking on the roads. Thankfully his bowels seemed to have settled down the last two days. At the edge of Ingleby Arncliffe Mal gently pottered on ahead and I was alone again with the promise of another long and painful day. Every step the pixie hammered the nail harder and firmer into my left kneecap, all the while chuckling and taunting as I grimaced and swore. I endured an unpleasant mile along the A172 before turning off at Swainby and heading into Scugdale. I passed, but only just, an elderly walker on one of the small climbs along the lane that wiggled its way carelessly up the valley, turning maliciously uphill then viciously down again as if trying to shake me off its back like a bucking bronco. On the climb up to Barkers Crags my average speed for the day so far was only five miles per hour. My head, heart and lungs, and even leg muscles were raring for faster, but the knee pixie had his foot firmly down on the brake and his six-inch nail rammed to the hilt under my patella. Standing for a moment and looking back over the flatlands of yesterday I was hit by a sudden idea. I pulled my phone from the backpack and began writing a text message. The text was to a good friend, Phil Clark, who was not only holidaying in Robin Hood's Bay and hoping to see our triumphant arrival, but more importantly is a pharmacist. I asked him what the maximum dose of painkillers was that I could take. Replacing my phone back in the pack I journeyed onwards, waiting for the beeps to tell me I had a reply. I didn't have to wait long, and I was surprised at his response. I could apparently take a lot more than I thought, and certainly more than I had swallowed the previous couple of days. One problem though, all the painkillers were in the car, so I diverted my mental focus away from my knee by using the fantastic scenery or concentrating on the map and navigation to ensure I would get to Seave Green.

On the descent from Barkers Crag I encountered three off-road motorbike riders. The first was attempting to drive up the steep, muddy rutted trail, and I stepped to the side as he wobbled and slid noisily past, filling the air with a sprayed mix of mud, shredded grass and petrol fumes. The other two sat on a wall next to their machines, one resting an arm on his sizeable belly whilst he puffed on a cigarette. Both looked uncomfortable and hot in their heavy dirt-laden leathers. The time was roughly half past ten in the morning and they looked exhausted. On seeing my approach the two stated that I "must be mad" to be running. I laughed and told them that I was running to Robin Hood's Bay, and they usefully stated "You'll not be there in time for lunch!" During a later conversation with Mal I learned he had a similar encounter with the same three guys. As he cycled past, the portly man at the rear asked him: "Is it easier on one of those, mate?" Mal just smiled back, but what he really wanted to say was "No, fat boy, you have an engine!"

The track descended and turned to the left before becoming a crude tarmac road that bisected the centre of a small hamlet, Raisdale Mill, through which flowed a pretty brook. Sprayed muddy tyre tracks indicated the off-road bikers had most likely passed this way. A further turn to the right and I was back on public roads again, with a tough uphill section immediately in front.

Concentrating on anything I could, other than the pain from my knee, I maintained good pace up the long incline, cresting the brow just as a road cyclist did the same from the opposite direction. He was evidently good at his sport. He had the appearance of a 'toasted whippet', consistent with many hard sun-baked hours on the bike, and was clad in matching lycra shorts and jersey. As he stood hammering on the pedals the bike rocked viciously from side to side, and his chest pulled hard for huge lungfuls of air. To him I must also have appeared to be running hard as we each nodded in mutual respect of the other's physical efforts.

Within a mile of Seave Green I called on the radio, hopeful that one of my colleagues would answer. Mal replied clearly, and occasionally crackly broken sounds of Andy's voice cut through. Mal had reached the village before the crew, passed straight through, and was now climbing up Medd Crag. Justin and Andy were yet to get there, having taken longer than expected to return from Richmond. I also reached the rendezvous before them and sat by the side of the road, deciding to wait for the drugs. Soon after, the crew car appeared and pulled off the road. Drugs! The dealers were here. It wasn't as if I was after crack cocaine or heroin, or even a shot of nandrolone. All I wanted was ibuprofen and co-codamol - two common over-the-counter pain remedies. But I wanted a lot of them, and in their own way they should make my knee hurt a lot less, and therefore enhance my performance. Performance enhancing drugs! Did this mean I was about to enter the filthy sordid world of the drugs cheat? Another glittering hopeful Olympic career shattered and ground into the dust alongside crushed ampoules and dirty syringes. Surely not! Although clearly not on a par with the perennial troubles encountered at events such as the Tour de France, what I was planning still didn't feel quite right. The 'Tour' has always fascinated me. Three-and-a-half thousand kilometres of cycling in three weeks, up and down ludicrously steep and high mountains in the Pyrenees and the Alps makes for the most extreme test of stamina and endurance of any mainstream sporting event. But, as a tour official once famously said, "You don't do this on mineral water and salad". Surely a reference to chemistry rather than the 8,000 or so calories per day that the competitors ingest legally. On many occasions amphetamine abuse has transformed riders into raging feral beasts, while the illicit use of EPO thickened blood to an extent that the heart struggled (sometimes to mortal failure) to exude the treacle-thick gloop through the vessels. Phil's text had come with a warning that, should I take the dose he'd said was safe, I could inflame my stomach. I was also aware that my knee was hurting for a reason, and simply to remove the pain and keep running would do nothing to help the cause of the pain, potentially contravening my 'no permanent damage' mantra. "But", I thought, "the time has come for pharmacological assistance". I put the tablets in my mouth, my knee in a daze (hopefully), my stomach and liver in hope, and my head in the sand. All washed down with a couple of fig roll biscuits before heading onwards up the hill behind Mal. Andy and Justin set off straight away for the second rendezvous to ensure this time they got there before the biker.

The climb up Medd Crag was short but steep, requiring a steady walk, however the gradient and slower pace produced a welcome reduction in pain, and checking the map I looked forward to getting on top of the moor and having a long, relatively flat section for several miles to Blakey Ridge. Over the last steep few metres of the climb I could see a wide gravel track heading very slightly uphill to the horizon about a mile away. This looked terribly inviting to increase my speed and I broke into a jog. Within half a dozen strides an excruciating sharp stabbing pain exploded from my knee down to my ankle and up to my hip and my left leg gave way underneath me. Crashing half to the ground, supported in a three-point crouch by my arms and right leg, I froze there, face contorted, trying to catch my breath. The pain slowly subsided! Rising back to my feet I walked a few tentative steps forward. The pain hadn't gone, but I could walk. Steadily I increased to a very slow jog, and then tried to push the pace again. Immediately there was a second electrifying lightning bolt through my leg and I was on the ground again. This wasn't good! It wasn't even bad. It was probably a disaster. As with the previous episode I stood upright, gathered myself and resumed walking. This time it remained a walk, any attempts at running were sure to strike me down with the same explosive surge of pain down the full length of my leg. A check of my GPS informed me that my best pace was now a pedestrian seventeen minutes per mile, which was immensely frustrating as the terrain was good for twice that speed. In my head I was still single-mindedly focused, automaton-like, on making it on foot all the way to Glaisdale, and began mental calculations, working out how long it would take to get there at the current speed, and what time in the evening I would arrive. I recalled a particular email I had received from Mad Dog after I suggested Vin and I might take spare bikes so we could continue by riding if we got too injured to run (a prophetic scenario in Vin's case). His response was unequivocal: "I think the back-up bikes may not be a good idea psychologically - it gives you a way out. I think you should 'burn the ships' and head inland with no means of retreat. If things get really bad, just make crutches out of fallen tree limbs, and hobble on. During training you should use good judgment, and avoid pain and injury at all costs. During endurance contests you should continue on as long as it is still possible to move. Taking part in ultra-endurance events has nothing to do with sanity. It has to do with pushing on regardless".

Several hill walkers appeared in the other direction as I plodded remorselessly on, my left foot turned very slightly outwards as I walked as this was more comfortable. Then a fell runner appeared, nodding to me as he passed and I felt a huge sense of disappointment, almost shame, my pride damaged by my inability to show him that I too was a runner. I wanted to shout to everybody that I was an ultra-marathoner, running from coast-to-coast, and that I would be tearing along if it weren't for my ungrateful, non-compliant knee. I yearned to yell after the runner "Race you!" or "Last one to the other side of the country is a big girl's blouse". But I said nothing. I was now on top of the hill, passing the trig point that marked the summit of Round Hill, a heathery and peaty moor in all directions. It occurred to me that if I strayed off the trail and collapsed due to a terminally malfunctioned knee joint that I might never be found, well, not for the next few thousand years at any rate - the preservative properties of peat bog have been proved numerous times with archaeological finds of whole petrified primitive people. I could have been dug up in a few millennia, prodded by scientists, and displayed in a museum to be gawped at by uncouth groups of future snotty-nosed schoolchildren. If I were luckier I could have a longer rest of a few million years or so, eventually fossilised and popping out of a Yorkshire cliff. At least this would mean I had finished my journey coast-to-coast, although I would have cheated - instead of grinding my way to the North Sea I'd have waited for it to grind its way to me. I imagined the conversation between alien paleontologists discovering me hanging half out of the cliff face.

"Blimey, Jeeves! Looks like an entire fossilized Homo sapiens from the late Quaternary period. Just before the mass extinction due to the McDonald's virus."

"You're right, Carruthers, but take a closer look at the legs. One of them is clearly designed to bend at the knee, whilst the other doesn't articulate at all. What an amazing discovery."

"Good Lord, so it is. I think we've found it! The missing link! Proof that ancient man evolved from forward-going dynamic creatures into idiots running round in circles. We'll be famous, we'll be rich beyond our wildest dreams."

"Load it into the space ship, Carruthers, but carefully now. Let's get it back to the lab on Andromeda".

Bizarre thoughts! Perhaps the crew had given me a few drugs too many.

Over the brow of Round Hill and Cockayne Head the trail turned gradually downwards towards the disused railway line that ran five miles to Blakey Ridge. Concerned that downhill had always been the more painful I found myself focussing on my knee, waiting for the expected increase in discomfort. It didn't come and I realised I actually had no pain. Anywhere!

I dared to start a jog, anticipating another thunderbolt striking me to the ground. No thunderbolt! A little faster and still I was pain free. Now on the level ground of the railway line not only was I pain free, but running free. A re-check of the GPS surprised me as I was beating eight minutes per mile, only feeling a general slight sluggishness at having 140 miles under my belt in the last five and a half days. There could be only one explanation – the drugs had kicked in. This was an opportunity to make up some lost time, and the next mile I timed at 7:50 before deciding that a slower pace was more sensible to prevent burnout and also minimise further knee damage. Running had become enjoyable again and I shifted my introspective focus back to the glorious surroundings of a high Yorkshire moor. Ahead of me in the east heavier cloud was building, under which hung a grey curtain of drizzle, sweeping ominously over the hills towards me. In comparison to the quieter trails, the disused railway line was something of a walker's motorway, and I passed ramblers every few hundred yards, all of whom were donning waterproofs in anticipation of the approaching rain.

The trail wound snake-like in a regular, almost sine-wave pattern as it followed the contours of the hillside round the heads of two stream-cut valleys. Four left sweeps, four right. I had been keeping a close eye on the map as I intended to take a tiny trail, 'Jackson's path', that headed straight over the moor near High Hill Top, cutting the corner between The Lion Inn at Blakey Ridge and the second rendezvous at Rosedale Head. Jackson's path is shown on the map as a dotted black line indicating it was very small and so could be difficult to find and follow. Approaching the point on the map I noticed a small cairn next to the railway line, adjacent to which was a thin track in the heather, no wider than seven or eight inches. Use of the compass confirmed it to be running in the correct direction, and I followed it, regularly checking the compass needle to ensure the direction was still correct.

Exactly as shown on the map the trail hit the road just north of the Lion Inn. I had now equalled the furthest point reached on my only previous coast-to-coast attempt. That was done as a walk with two friends as seventeen-year-olds. We carried a tent and all our equipment, which was too heavy for our youthful inexperienced bodies to try and haul the long distances we had hoped to cover. We had set up camp in a field next to the Lion Inn, one of the highest pubs in England. During the night a fierce storm blew in, shredding the tent, scattering our belongings over the moor and forcing us to seek refuge in the pub before calling parents to pick us up in the morning. We never made it to Robin Hood's Bay. My persisting memory of that attempt was one of pain, blisters and exhaustion, testament to our general lack of training, planning and experience. However, our enthusiasm to 'give it a go' couldn't be knocked.

On reaching the road I could see the crew car about three quarters of a mile ahead, parked on the roadside at a viewpoint. It started moving, and concerned that I was overdue and that they were about to leave, I radioed to tell them of my imminent arrival. On reaching Justin and Andy they explained that Mal had left them a few minutes earlier and had suggested they park in the Inn car park, as it would be a shorter distance for me to reach them. They were evidently unaware that I was planning to take Jackson's path. I only accepted a couple more fig roll biscuits, as I wanted to carry on whilst still in my drug-induced pain-free window, and also it was cold, drizzly and very windy at the checkpoint. I set off following the route taken by Mal, who had been with the crew quite some time. He had been suffering from cold and hunger having been caught out by the change in the weather and also having missed refuelling at Seave Green.

Ten minutes or so of road running was required to reach a long scenic bridleway that wound round the head of Great Fryup Dale, and was mostly slightly downhill. I thought I kept getting a glimpse of the sea but everything above the near horizon was too much the same shade of dull mid-grey to be certain. At several points I recognised Mal's tyre tracks in the softening mud and was sure he'd enjoyed riding this entertaining section. The trail was clearly marked every half mile or so with new-looking wooden posts upon which were carved 'coast to coast', and which offered a good opportunity for a photograph.

A hundred yards before the track reached the road high above Glaisdale I stepped to the side to allow a couple of waterproof-clad walkers to pass in the opposite direction. They asked me in a broad American drawl if it was far to the Lion Inn, and we chatted for a few minutes. They were a Californian couple, walking the coast-to-coast from east to west, and were very impressed when told of our week's running of the route. So impressed in fact that they insisted on taking my photograph so they could "talk about it to the folks back home".

The lane dropped very steeply down Caper Hill and twisted into the narrow river valley of Hardhill Gill. My gait was reduced to the occasional hop to save my knee. The more level terrain of Glaisdale side along the valley bottom provided the opportunity to increase the pace again for the last two or three miles to the bed and breakfast. I was still pain-free and back on a high, occasionally calling over the radio to anyone who might have been able to hear. Eventually Mal, who had just arrived at our accommodation, replied and provided me with accurate directions to the pub. He also wisely told me to slow down when I informed him that I was currently running at a pace faster than seven minutes per mile. Four hundred yards from the day's finish I received a call from the crew who had just arrived, saying that they had passed Vin and that he was nearly finished after his long day in the saddle. I turned to look behind me and there indeed was the cycling Dutchman, a hundred yards behind me. The race was on! Gradually my pace increased until I was nearly sprinting, but luck wasn't with me. The finish was downhill and my rival had mechanical advantage, easily passing me at speed before we both pulled to a stop, the full team together, outside the Arncliffe Arms. We had all arrived within fifteen minutes of each other, and there too was Ans who was excited at seeing her son finish a stage and also to now be involved with the event. Speaking perfect English but with a strong Dutch accent she introduced herself, never having met us before, and chatted enthusiastically to each one of us about our adventure. Vin visibly resembled Ans, and they shared an immensely likeable personality, although neither would have suited the other's hairstyle – his shaven crew cut, hers shoulder-length brown and curly. And Ans smelled nicer. Much nicer! After several days of testosterone sodden stale sweat, mud, Vaseline, old running shoes and bike grease (not to mention Vin's open air bowel habits), the clean perfumed scent of a woman was something to send the olfactory system into dizzying overdrive. It made us consider what an unpleasant odour we must have been dragging around with us wherever we went.

Once again everyone had done well. Mal completed a demanding ride in difficult conditions with no early support, Vin cycled around 50 road miles on an off-road bike, the crew had only missed Mal early on due to impossible time constraints, and my GPS told me I had covered 26.5 miles with 4000 feet of climbing in five hours exactly.

We sat outside the pub eating, drinking and chatting for a few minutes until the cold drizzle forced us inside. Ans, who was staying at a nearby bed and breakfast, arranged to meet us in the Arncliffe Arms for evening meal. Mal and I shared a small but comfortable twin room, the floor space just large enough to lay and stretch. And stretch I did, the drugs now having worn off and the pain in my left knee being more intense than I could ever have imagined.

Following an hour or two's rest I hopped down the stairs into the pub's restaurant where the six of us enjoyed the best food of the trip. The Arncliffe Arms has an excellent chef and the meal was quite fantastic. The landlady proudly told us that they try to offer the best quality food on the whole of the coast-to-coast route, and I would argue that they succeed.

Six days done, one to go! Surely we could crawl from here!

oooOooo

A Stones Throw

Day 7. Monday 15th May 2006. Glaisdale to Robin Hoods Bay.
17 miles

We woke to another wet rainy morning. No matter what happened, today it would all be over – either glorious success or devastating eleventh-hour failure. Which outcome would prevail was very much uncertain. The final day was a measly seventeen miles in distance with only a few small hills; comparatively easy. But when I eventually managed to get out of bed I was unable to walk.

The thought of finishing was a double-edged sword. Whilst finishing was what we had all trained for, and would bring a halt to the pain and suffering, it would also mean the joyride was over. Eighteen months of preparation, training and organisation and a week of high adventure condemned to memory and photographs, stories to be told around barbecues and campfires!

I knew the last hill down into Robin Hood's Bay very well and had visualised the finish a thousand times. Andy and Justin would roll gloriously down in the car to signal our imminent arrival to a group of family and friends who waited in the sunshine on the slipway by the Bay Hotel. Andy's radio would be beeping as we pressed our 'call' buttons without speaking, a signal to the waiting throng that we were almost home. Mal would ride down next, straight onto the sands and into the sea before abandoning his bike and hugging his girlfriend (also called Andrea). A moment later Vin and I would run into sight, appearing almost in slow motion as we effortlessly made the last few yards to our journey's end, families cheering and hugging us. It was always hot and sunny in my ending and we were running easily and pain-free. Always! I'd seen it so many times.

But this morning the rain hammered down, and I couldn't even walk.

Steeped in history and charm, it was hard to think of a more fitting place to finish our adventure than Robin Hood's Bay. Presumably Wainwright thought the same when he devised his now famous walk. Although tiny, Robin Hood's Bay is unable to expand due to geographical constraints, crammed as it is into a small steep and narrow river gorge, and is no bigger than it was two or three hundred years ago. It is situated five miles to the south of Whitby, the harbour town home of the great explorer Captain James Cook, and also where Bram

Stoker contrived Count Dracula's entry into England. Despite the name there is no evidence that Robin Hood of Sherwood Forest folklore ever visited the place; instead the name most probably derives from legends with local origins, as Robin Hood was the name of an ancient forest spirit. The present village originated somewhere in the 15th century, and by the 18th century was allegedly the busiest smuggling community on the Yorkshire coast. Its natural isolation, protected all around by moorland, aided the illicit business, which, despite its dangers, paid better than fishing. Hiding places, boltholes and secret passages abounded. It is said that a bale of silk could pass from the bottom of the village to the top without leaving the houses. Nowadays the village appears delightfully smeared through time, unable and unwilling to shake off its history but also keeping up to some degree with modern Britain. It has one foot in its fishing past and the other walking confidently into 21st century tourism; this being visibly demonstrated by pyramids of lobster pots piled up alongside small wooden fishing boats balanced near to trendy café bars that sell latte and skinniccino. Cobbled narrow alleyways retain the feel of a smugglers' haven, although now they weave between holiday cottages for let rather than housing locals.

Once again I had to hop downstairs to breakfast, unable to put my left foot to the floor comfortably. I couldn't fail now! Please don't let me fail now. I was sporting an elasticated bandage around my left knee to try and give it some support, and this did appear to help slightly. Sitting round the breakfast table enjoying more excellent food, Mal had a good idea, and I reached for my phone. Another text to Phil (now known as 'Phil the Pill') was hastily written:

"You told me the maximum painkillers I could take yesterday. Now tell me the REAL maximum."

Two minutes later the reply had arrived and I was swallowing enough tablets to anaesthetise a small elephant, all washed down with bacon on gipsy toast (the breakfast was as good as the evening meal). I was hoping to time it so that the start of the pain-free window would coincide with the start of the days running. Vin sat next to me, also taking painkillers, as his plan was to run again for the final day and his thigh was still painful. Mal had invited Justin to join him for the final day's cycling, but Justin hadn't been keen owing to the nasty weather. A few choice comments from the rest of us soon persuaded him to change his mind. With the car loaded and ready to go Andy had us posing in the lane for a final team photo shoot. The drugs had just started working for us two runners and we both urged Andy to get the pictures taken quickly so we could get started. Following the final group farewells and good lucks, we were off heading for the finish, and it all seemed a world away from the journey up to the Lake District exactly a week before.

oooOooo

Monday 8th May 2006. Chesterfield to St Bees Head.

Andy had arrived to collect me on time, which is unusual for a man who considers three-quarters of an hour late to be early! My bags loaded in the car, Andy set about putting Justin's bike, which had been stored in my garage since the practice run, on the roof of the car. Then there was the family farewell. This was a quietly emotional affair. Neither Andrea nor I wanting to appear too upset to the other as we kissed and hugged goodbye in the sunshine on the front lawn. I'd never spent a week away from Andrea since we were married over seven years previously, and I was also leaving four-year-old Hannah and five-month-old William with her. Despite having the focus of the coast-to-coast to occupy me, the absence of my family would leave a massive unfillable hole. Andrea had given me a framed photograph of the three of them, which I looked at proudly whenever possible.

The journey to St Bees began with a trip to Sheffield to pick up some T-shirts that Justin had arranged to be printed, before collecting the man himself and heading to the Hillsborough stadium to meet representatives from Red Bull. Andy had contacted the drinks company informing them of our attempt to run a marathon a day across the country, and they considered it crazy enough to provide us with some sponsorship. We easily found the 'Red Bull' Beetle car with a giant can of Red Bull on the roof, parked in the stadium car park, and inside sat two young women, Verity and Alex, who were to supply us with cases of the drink and take some pictures for their company promotion.

'Sat-nav Natalie' then directed us to Mal's house in Huddersfield, where he and Vin waited with several bags of food supplies for the week. Justin had also remarked how unusual it was for Andy to have been on time, but we both wished he hadn't mentioned it when the explanation was provided. To ensure an early start Andy had decided not to go to bed at all, instead staying awake all night. He informed us of this as he sped up the fast lane of the M1 motorway, downing his second can of Red Bull to help keep him awake.

After a quick lunch we all squeezed in the car. Just! Despite the borrowed roof box, space was severely limited and two stops *en route* were required to stretch our legs and change the seating arrangement. The atmosphere in the car was jolly despite almost sitting on each other's knees; the air conditioning played a major part in our comfort as the outside temperature rose steadily throughout the day.

On the M6 the visibility was excellent, and a noticeable nervous quietness invaded the car as the large, rocky ominous mountains of the Lake District came into view and we were suddenly reminded of the enormity of our challenge ahead, which up to this point had seemed much more frivolous.

The roads from Keswick to St Bees had been tortuous, but we finally made it and found the bed and breakfast easily with plenty of daylight to spare. Once settled the five of us took the steady half-mile walk in the mild evening sun to the sea and each chose a pebble from the shoreline, it being traditional when attempting the coast-to-coast to carry a stone from the Irish Sea to throw into the North Sea. I took four small stones, one for each member of my family, making certain to keep them safe in my Camelbak. Then it was the gentle stroll back for an early night, though I left Justin and Andy awake and tinkering with the laptop. My treasured family photograph was on the bedside table as I switched out the light, hoping for a relaxing and full nights sleep.

By nine o-clock the following morning we were standing once again on the pebbly beach, contemplating what might be to come and trying to visualise a challenging yet successful and hopefully pain-free crossing of the country.

oooOooo

Leaving Glaidsale via a muddy track that led behind the Arncliffe Arms into the woods it was clear that it had indeed been challenging, and the chances of success were currently looking good. 'Pain-free', however, was not an appropriate description, although Vin and I were both running comfortably under the influence of the drugs as we climbed up East Arncliffe wood, with Mal and Justin following behind. The heavy rain had greased the surface of the trail, with soft mud and wet moss covering slabs of stone that offered very little traction. This made biking treacherous and we pulled out a good lead on the cyclists as they slid and tumbled, before running down a steep lane to Egton Bridge. Once onto another flat disused railway line that runs down the Esk valley we were quickly caught and passed by first Mal then Justin, who were both splattered with mud. Their route took them high onto Sleights Moor and Blea Hill, whilst we decided to keep the running simple to avoid further injury, and took a bridleway that hung on the north side of Esk Dale towards Sleights. Several sections of this however, were, treacherous, the soil being predominantly clay that clogged the tread of our shoes and was as slippery as ice on the short steep climbs and descents.

From the valley bottom at Sleights we ran hard along a road to Ruswarp, trying to cover as much distance as possible before the drugs wore off, and indeed we ran the fastest mile of the whole coast-to-coast on this section. After crossing the river Esk and climbing up a steep winding lane we took another old railway line that headed southeast towards our agreed rendezvous point at High Hawsker. Despite appearing flat the track had a fatiguing incline, which, after we had run for the previous six days, required us to dig deep into our physical and mental resources to keep moving. After two-and-a-half miles of it we were at High Hawsker, climbing up the embankment, over a stile and along a farm track to the pub. The team was to regroup here before Justin joined Andy again, leaving Mal, Vin and myself to complete the final three or four miles to Robin Hood's Bay. A pub was chosen as a suitable checkpoint in case we had to wait for our welcoming party to get to the finish. Andrea was driving up with Hannah and William with Mal's Andrea, and my parents were making the journey over from Keswick. They all wanted to see us arrive so it was vital we didn't get there first.

Vin and I were first to the pub, and whilst we stood in the road waiting for the others my parents happened to drive by, saw us and stopped. They were very pleased to see us and took a quick photo before offering encouragement and driving off to our destination.

Concerned about the absence of Andy and Ans (although Ans' car was parked at the pub) we called on the radio to be told that they were waiting for us to appear from another trail that they believed we were taking several miles to the south. On realising the mistake they headed to meet us, and arrived a few minutes later. The grey skies were getting angrier and the temperature cooler, and Vin and I kept jogging round the car park to keep warm and prevent stiffness whilst we snacked. A beep from inside my Camelbak announced the arrival of a text message – the Andreas and children had parked up at the top of the hill in Robin Hood's Bay and were making their way down to the Bay Hotel. With the welcoming party in place we were free to set off to the finish, but still waited for the arrival of Mal and Justin. They were taking some time, and we were both worried that we would come out of our pain-free period, and also that the weather was steadily worsening. Although only a mile or so from the sea we still hadn't seen it due to low clouds and rain. With a sense of humour still intact though, I asked Andy to find a thick black pen, and he drew a smiling face on the bandage covering my infernal knee. Every time I took a step the shape of the bandage changed and the smile widened to a grin.

The bikers eventually arrived, completely covered in mud. The moors had been a sloppy mess, causing some crashes and slowing them down considerably. Justin had lost his radio in one such crash in the difficult conditions. He quickly loaded his bike on the car. Mal agreed to continue immediately, as he too was keen to finish. Ans and the support crew waved us off one last time and they drove towards the final rendezvous at the top of the hill at Robin Hood's Bay, while Mal, Vin and I sped back to the railway line, the three of us staying together until we runners took a path that went straight down the steep hillside through a caravan park at Hawsker Bottom to the cliff edge. A dull mid-grey mass that was the North Sea finally sprawled below us, not looking at all inviting as the rain and wind roughed its surface into a boiling foam. Running the fierce downhill gradient to the cliff path was a battle for us both and, in hindsight, a bad mistake as we were both dragged out of our relative comfort and thrust back into our respective agony. We took the painkillers together and our pain-free period ended together, with less than three miles to go. Had we stayed on the railway line we would likely have been at the top of the village by now. Instead we had to negotiate a difficult slippery cliff path that wound round the headland of Ness Point and had several short but steep climbs and descents, every 'up' reducing us to a walk and each 'down' a painful treacherous one-legged hop. Our pain rapidly worsened, and for both of us it was now more severe than at any time during the previous days. I was quickly on the radio calling for any team-mate who could hear to come to our aid with more painkillers. Nobody replied and we hobbled woefully onwards, occasionally surprising the odd walker as we passed, they being unable to hear our approach as they were wrapped fully in waterproofs with hoods pulled tightly around their ears. The wind blew, the rain pummelled and our legs stung so fiercely we could barely move. This wasn't how it was supposed to end. I'd seen the glorious final flourish many times and this definitely wasn't it! At least the face on my knee bandage kept grinning.

Although radio reception was very crackly, Mal eventually answered our calls for assistance and he, having painkillers in his pack, agreed to come and meet us on the cliff path. We had hobbled a further half-mile or so before he came into view, pushing (not riding) his bike along the 'walkers only' trail. As we swallowed some ibuprofen he told us that he had taken his bike all the way across the country with no trouble, yet when walking ten yards with it along the cliff path he had been shouted at by a local, telling him in no uncertain terms that he shouldn't have been there. For our benefit Mal ignored the man in his garden and carried on regardless. The reduction in our speed had delayed our arrival at the finish, so a text message was sent to the welcoming party informing them we would be a few minutes longer.

A few minutes was all it took as we were only 400 yards from the car park at the top of Robin Hood's Bay where Andy, Justin and Ans were waiting for us, Ans relieved and quite emotional to see Vin hobbling down the street towards her. She gave him a big hug as we regrouped before, as planned, sending the crew down the last hill into town first. Mal went a minute later, followed immediately by Vin, Ans, and myself, Ans shouting encouragement as she ran alongside us. The ridiculously steep gradient of the road down to the village bottom made for impossible running with our injuries, and we both adopted a kind of hop / skip technique that drew curious looks from the swarm of schoolchildren that buzzed around the narrow streets (evidently Robin Hood's Bay is popular with school field trips!). Very steep but thankfully short, the hill was descended within a minute, replaced by a narrow level section that I knew well; round two easy bends and only a hundred yards to the beach. I couldn't see them yet but I knew my family were waiting near the slipway, and suddenly my existence plunged into a kind of sensory slow motion; I can't remember hearing any sounds, I had no idea where Vin was (he was actually a few yards behind me), I felt no pain, and I knew I was about to cry.

It was strawberry flavour! The first thing I saw as the tears started. Pink ice cream held in Hannah's left hand as she fluttered around Andrea's feet like a wind-blown butterfly. Behind them stood my parents and Mal's Andrea, all looking back towards the bottom of the hill. Andrea bent down next to Hannah, still holding the umbrella to shield them both from the rain, and pointed towards me some 30 yards away. I remember hearing the shout of "Daddy", and felt my face contort with trying to stem the flood of tears and emotions that threatened to burst me like an overfilled balloon. I ran and bent down next to Hannah and asked for a lick of her ice cream. She refused, and yelled a loud "Hey!" as I stole one anyway, before picking her up and planting a big teary kiss on her cheek. Putting her back down again I grabbed Andrea, who was also looking overcome, before she let me go, telling me that I hadn't finished yet and gestured towards the beach. Turning to jog the final yards I remembered I hadn't been suffering the last week alone, and wondered where the rest of the team were. At the slipway stood Justin and Andy, who held his big video camera. I asked where the car was and Andy replied "There!" pointing towards the sea. The crew car had been driven down the slipway and onto the sand; the front wheels in seawater signifying that it had also truly made it from coast-to-coast. On the roof stood Justin's bike, dirty but proud, and www.RespectTheStupidity.com emblazoned across the back window stared back at the full entourage who now congregated on the slipway, handing out paper cups of champagne. To the left of the car in the shallow surf lay Mal's bike, ridden and dumped into the sea, as he promised, while Mal received a hug from his Andrea behind us. A hugging epidemic began, with everyone involved – the team, wives, girlfriends, parents, children, even Phil the Pill and his wife Sheena who had watched the drama unfold from the steps of the old coastguard station in which they were staying for the week. My father organised the five of us into a group in front of a small fishing boat next to the slipway and the photo's began as we stood together, arm in arm and beaming like crazed idiots. People were taking pictures from all angles, flashes popping like fireworks on bonfire night, and we had the feeling of film stars in front of the paparazzi. Phil climbed onto the coastguard station balcony, popped open a bottle of champagne and sprayed it down onto us, accompanied by cheers. Next to us stood William's pram in which he lay, sleeping soundly through the uproar.

Today we had covered seventeen miles in three hours and five minutes. But the final task was still to de done, and I hobbled down onto the wet sands and headed over flat rocks to the closest section of incoming waves accompanied by the rest of the team, Andrea and Hannah, my father and Phil. The five of us stood in the sea for some further photo's before reaching into our packs and retrieving the pebbles collected from St Bees Beach. Andrea placed one in William's hand for a few seconds whilst he slept, before throwing it and then her own into the surf. Hannah was next, but after her throw she wanted another go so I fetched the pebble back for her to have a second attempt. Finally it was my turn and I threw with all my might, watching the small symbol of a week's toil and torment arc effortlessly through the leaden sky and into the sea with barely a sound or ripple. We'd covered 173 miles in 32 hours and 34 minutes of running, walking, hobbling and limping - climbing and descending roughly 24,000 feet. We had finished.

oooOooo

Vin approaching the summit of Nine Standards Rigg

Matt and Vin suffering near Keld

Approaching the rendezvous just after Jackson's Path

Justin's bike, dirty at last

The last few yards

End of an adventure

Finished!

Epilogue

We all milled around aimlessly on the beach for a few minutes until the damp coldness started to penetrate our armour of triumph, and our gathered friends and relatives ushered us to the convoy of cars waiting to escort us to Raven Hall. The moors were heavily shrouded in a thick blanket of mist for the short drive to the hotel, and after a week of faultless map and compass navigation across the country my driver and navigator misplaced us trying to follow the correct roads to our destination. The accommodation, and food therein, was magnificent and we spent two days recuperating (although my family and I suffered sleepless nights at the hands of a nasty stomach bug contracted by Hannah, and also William's nocturnal demands for feeds) before leaving for our respective homes.

Re-integration to normal life was difficult after the adventure and camaraderie, but Andrea was very glad to have me back. It took two weeks before I was able to walk downstairs properly. Up until then my knee would only allow me to put my left leg down on the next step, my right leg joining it on the same level rather than going down further. Three months post-coast-to-coast I could only do some short distance (up to five miles) running, only slowly at first but later up to my previous 10K race speed. Fortunately the knee was no problem when riding a bike or swimming so I had been getting my necessary fix of endurance exercise via these sports.

During post-event email conversations with Mad Dog he told me that, had I been able to contact him after the knee trouble started, he might have been able to help me prevent it worsening, and indeed, by following the advice he subsequently offered, I *was* soon running pain-free once more. He also told me that what we did was more than simply an ultra-distance run; it was "A true adventure to rival those of the pioneers of old".

Any regrets from the adventure? Absolutely none at all!

Would I do it again?

Definitely, yes, it was 'Brilliaaaaant'.

Would I do anything different?

I'd try harder to contact Mad Dog in the event of any injury to get his expert advice.

Five months after the event I completed a half marathon race, knocking six minutes off my previous best time for thirteen miles, and finishing well inside 90 minutes (it had been a long-term ambition of mine to run the distance in less than an hour and a half). It would seem from this result that my mantra of 'no permanent damage' was, thankfully, successful.

Shortly after returning home Andy met Mal in the Peak District to record some video of him riding with the mini-camera attached to his bike. The bike had been revitalised; fully serviced by a mechanic who furrowed his brow and shook his head in despair when told of its complete immersion in the North Sea. Salt water may be used as a preservative, but not for steel. After successfully riding off road the full width of the country without so much as a minor incident Mal had a major crash on the first post-event ride, smashing his helmet and breaking his collar bone. The only upside to this being that the bike mounted camera was running, catching the crash on video up to the point of blank screen as the impact hit fully. Conspiracy theorists have cast doubt over whether it was a true accident or if he 'took a dive', as he was signed off work throughout the 2006 football World Cup, and it wasn't his drinking arm that was affected. A full ten sunny but inactive weeks of lying on the floor later his collarbone still refused to 'stick together', although his doctors had put him out of some of the misery of boredom by allowing him to drive and work again. A further four months was predicted before he could ride a bike again.

Vin's thigh muscle healed fully in just a few days. So much so in fact that he ran the Chester half-marathon five days after finishing the coast-to-coast. Being used to running for several hours at a time he found the race disappointingly short, and although posting an excellent time it was still, not surprisingly, several minutes slower than his personal best. Then he went away for Police training, as he was successful in his application to join the force. He was looking forward to wearing his heavy stab-vest and police equipment all day, stating it would be "Good training". Good luck to any criminals who fancy their chances of out-running him!

Our excellent support crew, Andy and Justin, being ever adaptable returned without fuss to 'normal' activities, although both admitted to feeling a sense of disappointment that the adventure was over. Several hours of video footage and still images remain to be viewed and tinkered with in Andy's editing suite to complete the video log of the event for posterity. The crew car survived without damage or malfunction and is still going strong, still proudly displaying its

RespectTheStupidity rear-window sticker. Justin's bike has returned to a life of inactivity as an elaborate dust-collecting ornament.

Following a few weeks poring over the food diary that he had kept, Justin was forthcoming with the data regarding our calorific intake throughout the event. Unfortunately, due to the excitement and relief of finishing, we had forgotten to record all we had eaten on the final day. However, from arriving in St Bees Head until leaving Glaisdale I had consumed a total of approximately 31,000 kcalories – roughly 5,000 kcalories per day, a value equivalent to twice the normal daily intake for a man. Surprisingly it wasn't the long second day that produced my highest food intake, but the first day to Rosthwaite when I allegedly consumed 6,100 kcalories*See Appendix 2. In an email to Mal and Vin I proclaimed myself the winner of the calorie competition as Mal's total for the week was 24,900 kcalories, and Vin, despite his apparent huge appetite, only managed a measly 21,600.

At the time of writing it is believed that we managed to raise somewhere near £500 for the Children In Need charity. The website www.respectthestupidity.com is still active and will be updated to accommodate future team events. This can surely mean one thing – we aren't stopping here. With a team get-together and barbecue scheduled for July 2006, alcohol-fuelled discussions are certain to involve the subject of "what next?"

What next indeed?

oooOooo

APPENDIX

1. Itinerary

Approximate distances run and altitude climbed were as follows:

Day 1. St Bees Head to Rosthwaite. 25 Miles. 3000 Feet.

Via Nannycatch, Ennerdale Bridge, Ennerdale Water, Black Sail Hut, Honister Hause, Peat Howe.

Day 2. Rosthwaite to Bampton. 26 Miles. 7800 Feet.

Via Birketts Leap, Watendlath, Blea Tarn, Wythburn, Raise Beck, Grizedale Tarn, Patterdale, Angle Tarn, Satura Crag, The Knott, High Raise, High Kop, Bampton Common.

Day 3. Bampton to Kirkby Stephen. 22 Miles. 3000 Feet.

Via Bampton Grange, Out Scar, Little Strickland, Wyegill Plantation, Crosby Ravensworth, Bank Moor, Hollin Stump, Asby Grange, Soulby.

Day 4. Kirkby Stephen to Reeth. 23 Miles. 3000 Feet.

Via Hartley, Hartley Fell, Nine Standards Rigg, Whitsundale, Keld, Swinner Gill, High Whim, Gunnerside Beck, Hard Level Gill, Surrender Bridge, Healaugh.

Day 5. Reeth to Ingleby Cross. 33 Miles. 1500 Feet
.

Via Grinton, Eddy's Bridge, Thorpe Under Stone, Richmond, Anchorage Hill, Brompton-on-Swale, Scorton, Bolton-on-Swale, Whitwell, Streetlam, Danby Wiske, Oaktree Hill, Deighton, Sydal Lodge.

Day 6. Ingleby Cross to Glaisdale. 26.5 Miles. 4000 Feet.

Via Swainby, Huthwaite, Scugdale Hall, Barkers Crag, Raisedale Mill, Seave Green, Round Hill, Bloworth Crossing, Farndale Moor, Rosedale Head, Great Fryup Head, Caper Hill, Glaisdale Side.

Day 7. Glaisdale to Robin Hood's Bay. 17 Miles. 1600 Feet.

Via East Arncliffe Wood, Egton Bridge, Priory Farm, Newbiggin Hall Farm, Groves Hall, Ruswarp, Stainsacre, High Hawsker, Hawsker Bottom, Ness Point.

Total 172.5 Miles. 23,900 Feet.

2. My food intake, day 1, St Bees Head to Rosthwaite:

High carbohydrate drink – 2 litres
Protein and carbohydrate drink – 1 litre
Orange juice
Corn flakes
Porridge
Scrambled eggs and bacon on toast
Malt loaf – 2 slices
Bananas – one and a half
Flapjack – one and a half
Jellybeans – 2 handfuls
Dextrose tablets – 2
Bagel with peanut butter
Scrummy – 75g
Dried apricots – 5
Chocolate raisins – 1 handful
Sports energy bar
Vegetable soup
Bread roll
Steak
Potatoes
Mixed vegetables

Printed in the United Kingdom
by Lightning Source UK Ltd.
130475UK00002B/388-390/A